CRASH BOAT

Lieutenant Earl A. McCandlish AUTHORS' COLLECTION

CRASH BOAT

Rescue and Peril in the Pacific During World War II

EARL A. McCANDLISH AND
GEORGE D. JEPSON

LYONS
PRESS

Essex, Connecticut

An imprint of Globe Pequot, the trade division of
The Rowman & Littlefield Publishing Group, Inc.
4501 Forbes Blvd., Ste. 200
Lanham, MD 20706
www.rowman.com

Distributed by NATIONAL BOOK NETWORK

British Library Cataloguing in Publication Information available

Library of Congress Control Number: 2020953023

ISBN 978-1-4930-5923-2 (hardcover : alk. paper)
ISBN 978-1-4930-7235-4 (paper : alk. paper)
ISBN 978-1-4930-5924-9 (e-book)

∞™ The paper used in this publication meets the minimum requirements of American National
Standard for Information Sciences—Permanence of Paper for Printed Library Materials, ANSI/
NISO Z39.48-1992.

To the wonderful people of Augusta, Kansas—many long gone, but all truly patriotic Americans—who gave their pennies, nickels and dimes to help bring about the birth of our crash boat, the P-399.
—EAM

In loving memory of my mother and father.
—GDJ

Contents

INTRODUCTION

THE JAPANESE ATTACK ON PEARL HARBOR ON DECEMBER 7, 1941, changed an American generation forever. Young men and women starting their lives, whether in the labor force or attending colleges and universities across the country, suddenly found themselves in the nation's armed services or working in wartime industries. Personal lives were on hold for the duration.

Although storm clouds had been on the horizon since the late 1930s, and Great Britain had been fighting for its very life against Nazi Germany, Americans had gone about their business, hoping to avoid war. While politicians debated a position of isolationism, and President Franklin D. Roosevelt found ways to support the British, there were strong signals that Japan was moving toward armed conflict with the US.

The air raid on Pearl Harbor, Hawaii, brought everything into the open, and sixteen million Americans faced the greatest challenge of the twentieth century. By early 1942, America was beginning to respond. Lines formed at recruiting stations as young men enlisted in various branches of the military.

Earl A. McCandlish was working in New York City, waiting for a US Navy commission to be confirmed when the war began. "Greetings" from Uncle Sam in early 1942 superseded his Navy application, and he was soon wearing an Army uniform, completing Officer Candidate School in Virginia.

As war engulfed the globe, aircraft flew over vast stretches of the oceans en route to targets and returning to bases. Rescuing downed pilots and flight crews at sea was a significant challenge. Unfortunately, there was little agreement among the services as to who was responsible overall for air-sea rescue and how to carry it out. Surface vessels of all sizes, submarines, and amphibious aircraft worked to recover downed pilots and aircrews without a clear plan of operation. Patrol boats of assorted sizes and converted military and civilian vessels were used, but these were not explicitly designed for the task, and each had its weaknesses.

In 1942 and 1943, a program to build air-sea rescue craft called "crash boats," officially designated as aircraft rescue vessels (AVR), was started. A standard design for a sixty-three-foot boat to be used by the Navy, Army, and Coast Guard was developed by a young naval architect named Dair Long who worked for the Miami Shipbuilding Company. Construction of the swift, sleek boats began in shipyards across the country.

At the same time, officers to command these vessels and crews to operate them funneled into training programs at the Higgins Boat Operators and Marine Engine Maintenance School in New Orleans. Instruction revolved around classroom sessions and hands-on experience aboard boats on Lake Pontchartrain and in the Gulf of Mexico.

US Army Air Force (AAF) Lieutenant Earl A. McCandlish arrived at the Higgins School as an instructor commanding the P-100, a cumbersome 110-foot-long antique from World War I, designed initially as a minesweeper. By autumn 1943, he was assigned command of a new AVR 63, then under construction at the Fellows & Stewart shipyard in Wilmington, California, near Long Beach. Along with his first permanent crew, he climbed aboard a train and headed west.

The new crash boats were developed along lines similar to Navy PT boats, though smaller in length by some seventeen feet. Designed for speed and maneuverability, they were outfitted with medical facilities for treating rescued pilots and flight crews. These boats also carried twin .50-caliber machine-gun turrets flanking the bridge and a single .50-caliber weapon in the stern cockpit.

Although designated as rescue boats, they also were frequently used as gunboats in both the Pacific and European theaters during the war. With graceful lines, they were pleasing to the eye and a joy to operate, skimming along at speeds over forty knots, powered by two Hall-Scott 630-horse engines. Their maneuverability was an asset in performing rescues and combat operations.

A lieutenant commanded each boat and a crew of six. The P-399 crew, including my father, George L. Jepson, represented cities and small towns across America and even the Netherlands.

Crash Boat is Earl McCandlish's story of the P-399—later named the *Sea Horse*—and the young men, recent civilians, who did their best to perform a humanitarian mission within parameters dictated by war. By VJ Day in 1945, the *Sea Horse* had plucked more than thirty airmen from the sea.

Earl McCandlish's memoir relates incidents the P-399 crew experienced that nearly eighty years later may seem harsh in depicting the Japanese. These passages reflect the raw reality of life in the Pacific war zone through the *Sea Horse* crew's lens at the time. There is no intent to disparage the Japanese people today.

Over a period of approximately eighteen months in the Southwest Pacific, the P-399 endured nightly Red Alerts (Japanese air attacks), survived typhoons, searched for and rescued downed Allied flyers, dropped agents on enemy-controlled islands, and provided humanitarian aid to Filipinos.

According to Lawrence (Bud) Waggener, Jr., who skippered the P-401 called *Gung-Ho* in the 15th Emergency Rescue Boat Squadron, the *Sea Horse* was the most decorated AAF rescue boat to serve in the Pacific.

—*George D. Jepson*

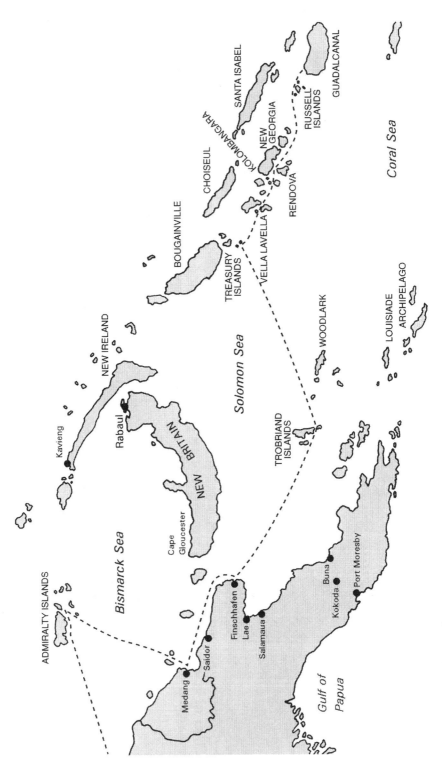

Path of the *Sea Horse* - 1 AUTHORS' COLLECTION

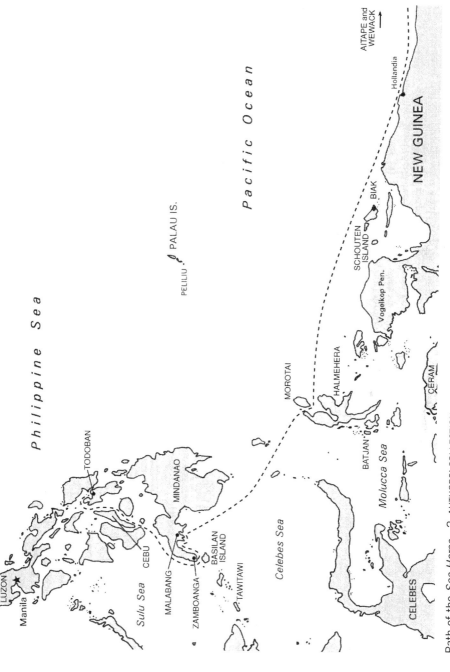

Path of the *Sea Horse* - 2 AUTHORS' COLLECTION

New Orleans

ON A MAY MORNING IN 1944, LIGHT RAIN FELL UNDER LOW SCUDDING clouds as the Liberty ship *James J. Corbett* steamed slowly into the Sealark Channel, part of a small convoy bound for Guadalcanal. *Corbett,* named for the American boxer best known for defeating John L. Sullivan, was positioned in the convoy's "coffin corner," the last ship in the last lane.

Our sixty-three-foot USAAF air-sea rescue boat, the P-399, was secured across a cargo hatch. During our 4,500-mile voyage across the Pacific from San Francisco, our eight-man crew lived aboard the crash boat, which we later named *Sea Horse.* Our sister boat, P-400, was made fast across another hatch.

As we finished breakfast in the ship's mess, Navy gun crews on the bow and stern opened fire. The call of "general quarters, general quarters . . . all hands man your battle stations" sent us scurrying on deck. The sound of watertight doors slamming shut echoed through the ship. A Navy destroyer screening the convoy charged by us, belching smoke, its loud, high-pitched "whoop, whoop, whoop," alarm piercing the air.

A lookout on the bridge wing had spotted the telltale wake of a periscope in the water. *Corbett* lurched into a zigzag pattern along with the other ships in convoy, while the escorting destroyers stalked the suspected Japanese submarine. Some of our crew had volunteered to man guns. Others stood by the rail, watching the destroyers while our hearts beat a little faster. After a relaxing, uneventful cruise across the Pacific, reality struck—this was a war zone.

Until the Japanese attacked Pearl Harbor on December 7, 1941, we were all civilians, enjoying the best years of our lives. In my early thirties, I was the "old man" and skipper aboard the *Sea Horse*. The rest of the crew were in their twenties. Over several months, we had bonded while shaking down the boat off the California coast.

Guadalcanal, the lush green and mountainous island where American forces had taken the offensive to the Japanese less than two years earlier, appeared through the mist. It was our first overseas station, assigned to the recently formed 15th Emergency Rescue Boat Squadron in support of the 13th Air Force with two other sixty-three-foot crash boats and a 110-foot supply boat. Naturally, we were anxious and, perhaps, a bit apprehensive.

After landing at Lunga Point, we learned the destroyers had sunk the Japanese submarine, one of eight chalked up by the US Navy that month in the Solomon Islands. The threat of an enemy torpedo attack was our welcome to the Southwest Pacific.

Over a year earlier, my journey to the war zone had begun not far from Bourbon Street and the French Quarter in New Orleans. In early spring 1943, I, as a newly commissioned lieutenant in the USAAF, drove my late-model, light blue Plymouth from New York to the Crescent City. My orders were to report for duty as an instructor at the Higgins Boat Operators and Marine Engine Maintenance School.

As I drove across the Lake Pontchartrain Causeway in southern Louisiana, I wondered what might lie ahead in this city famous for its cuisine and jazz. Little did I know that within a few months I would be sitting down to dinner with headhunters on an island in the South Pacific. For the moment, however, I was only concerned about my immediate future.

On the morning following my arrival in New Orleans, I reported to headquarters where operations welcomed me with little formality, assigning me as skipper of the P-100, docked on the lake at the Southern Yacht Club near the US Navy training base. Naively, I took this all in stride as a freshly minted second lieutenant.

The school charged us with training new skippers to run, navigate, and command air-sea rescue boats. Instruction was to focus on dead reckoning, celestial navigation, and boat handling. I couldn't believe the school had given me this responsibility. Arriving at the yacht club, I was bowled over when I saw that my boat was 110 feet long. The P-100 was initially designed by the Navy as a subchaser, or salvage vessel, during World War I.

Aghast, I resolved to make it clear to the commanding officer that I was only qualified to instruct trainees in navigation—not how to command this relic from the Great War. I had completed a course in navigation at the Hayden Planetarium in New York City during 1941 and 1942. The Navy had set up the school, using the planetarium to teach star identification. Since this was in my official record, it explained my assignment as an instructor.

My only previous boat-handling experience had been on Lake Champlain in upstate New York, occasionally steering the sixty-foot yacht *Linwood II* during the summer of 1935. The yacht belonged to the Ruppert family, owners of the Knickerbocker Brewery and the New York Yankees Baseball Club. Each week we sailed from Valcour Island, near Ticonderoga, to Burlington, Vermont, for supplies.

That same summer, I helped search for Benedict Arnold's Revolutionary War gunboats that had sunk in the lake during the Battle of Valcour Island on October 11, 1776. Under the direction of Captain Lorenzo Hagglund , who learned about the battle while stationed on the lake during World War I, another fellow and I did a controlled bottom search, dragging a chain between two twenty-two-foot Chris-Craft runabouts, hoping to find one of the historic vessels.

One day we snagged the *Philadelphia*, the first American gunboat discovered, which now rests in the Smithsonian Institution in Washington, DC. In the summer of 1997, the Lake Champlain Maritime Museum found additional boats in Arnold's flotilla using modern technology.

My time at *Linwood II*'s helm and steering a runabout hardly qualified me for handling a 110-foot vessel. Fortunately, I met the skipper from one of the P-100's sister ships as I was leaving the dock for the first time. Hank, a warrant officer, was an experienced Mississippi River tugboat captain. After enlisting in the AAF, he volunteered for the boat company, wanting to serve on the water.

Hank always had stubble on his face, and his overall appearance was one of a slept-in bed. Except for his southern accent, he could have passed for a New England fisherman. We got along fine from the start. That first day, we sat on the afterdeck of the P-100, jawing about our assignments. Both of us were apprehensive about our new duties.

Unsettled about teaching navigation, he had no problem with boat-handling instruction. His only navigation experience was paying attention to buoys and taking bearings on known points up and down the river, but his knowledge of tides, currents, and winds was invaluable. I was confident he could sail a boat anywhere there was a light rain or heavy dew. Still, he knew little about dead reckoning and nothing about celestial navigation or star identification.

Hank suggested we swap knowledge. So, in the days ahead, before the first trainees arrived, he taught me about bridge duties, engine room signaling, lines, anchoring, and much more. I instructed him in primary navigation: the laying of compass courses, estimation of speed, use of a tachometer, time of departure, estimated time of arrival, use of nature's signs, and seat-of-the-pants calculated guesses. Using star charts, he learned star identification and about the constellations, planets, sun, moon, and major and minor stars.

Absorbing everything in a brief time was a challenge. There were only eleven days before the first group of trainees would arrive. After agreeing to assist each other, Hank suggested that we fuel the P-100 the next morning and take it out on Lake Pontchartrain. He knew a fellow at the yacht club who would work in the engine room for a few dollars. I hoped I could learn enough to get by.

Early the next morning, we picked up our engine-room man and went to the yacht club. Fueling took about two hours. Then we went out about a mile on the lake, where Hank instructed me in engine and throttle control, backing, turning, and steering. A light breeze and low choppy waves allowed me to feel the wind on the boat's high bow. Every twenty minutes, we took a break for our engine room man. Working the clutches was demanding work. After five days, particularly docking and undocking, I developed a feel for the boat.

Meanwhile, I taught Hank to set a course for Slidell across Lake Pontchartrain, which is about twenty-eight miles wide. I set the throttle for nine knots, against a slight crosswind. He was so pleased when he made landfall. As our mutual instruction continued, Hank caught on to dead reckoning and finally told me that it was as easy as "pouring piss out of a boot with the directions written on the side." He had a colorful way of expressing himself.

During the days waiting for the trainees to arrive, we practiced and practiced. I wondered what people on the shore, the causeway, or other boats must have thought about our maneuvers. On a couple of clear nights, we gazed at stars and planets, while Hank learned how to determine his location.

The first trainees, most in their early twenties, finally reported. I was over thirty and felt old. There were twenty-two to twenty-five assigned to each boat; new lieutenants were trained to command boats, and the enlisted men to serve as mates (second in command for deck duties) and seamen. Operations furnished instructors for medical technicians and ordnance and picked engineers to train engine room oilers.

Each week, trainees received three hours of classroom instruction, allowing me to teach an abbreviated course on celestial navigation. The lessons covered using the transit, the almanac, and chronometer and taking sun and moon shots.

Onboard demonstrations followed classroom instruction. Overall, it only provided the basic background necessary for lieutenants to command their own boats. We encouraged everyone to continue studying navigation because of its importance to their immediate future at sea. Hank was relieved he didn't have to teach navigation complexities. Surprisingly, the first class went well with no mishaps.

Among the trainees, we found fine crewmen who would eventually sail aboard the P-399. Danny Tholenaars, a Dutch national and a veteran seaman, was exceptional. His father taught him to sail on the Zuider Zee at the age of six. He had spent more time on the water than he had on land. As a young man, Danny became the quartermaster on a Dutch freighter.

Early in the war, his ship was unloading cargo on the Surrey Commercial Docks in Rotherhithe, South East London, when the Luftwaffe suddenly appeared. A small bomb landed on the freighter's deck but didn't explode. Danny quickly scooped it up and tossed it into the Thames. It went off, inflicting only minor damage to the ship. The Netherlands's Queen Wilhemina decorated him for this act of bravery.

Once back at sea in the Atlantic, Danny was again decorated when a German U-boat torpedoed and sank the freighter he was on. When a German submarine torpedoed his next ship off Nova Scotia, rescuers sent him to Boston, where he stayed briefly in a military hospital. While visiting friends in Michigan, the brave Dutchman volunteered for military service, even though he was in the country illegally. Based on his previous experience, the AAF assigned him to the Higgins School.

Danny joined my training crew and came with me to the P-399 after leaving the Higgins School. Three other trainees, Homer Baker, Adam Taylor, and Wilson Hollis, each outstanding in his respective military occupational specialty (MOS), also headed to the West Coast after graduation, assigned to the P-399.

Once the first two classes completed the training course, they were assigned to new boat crews. Those who washed out were sent to non–crash boat units. New skippers, along with their deck and engine crews, received orders to sail their boats from the Southern Yacht Club to one of four coastal ports: Biloxi, Mississippi; Pensacola, Florida; Fort Meyers, Florida; or Brownsville, Texas.

Crews practiced their newly learned skills en route: boat handling, navigating, engineering, signaling, radio operations, galley duty, and medical procedures for downed pilots and injured personnel. Although these missions helped prepare us for the real thing, the war and live combat situations seemed a long way off.

After spending the night in their respective ports, each boat was directed to a predetermined latitude and longitude in the Gulf of Mexico and given the estimated arrival time. Trainers did not offer advice. The hope was for fair weather, but severe storm forecasts scrubbed missions. It was surprising how well the crews performed—a tribute to American adaptability.

We frequently created new drills for the medics, but one real incident almost become a tragedy as we returned to New Orleans on our third training voyage. Cruising westward in the Gulf of Mexico on a warm day, we were making about eight knots in calm seas. Suddenly, as the port watch went off duty, they screamed from below in the crew quarters that the starboard watch was either dead or dying.

I rushed below and ordered unaffected crewmen to bring the stricken men on deck. Fresh air and artificial respiration soon had them coughing, wheezing, and vomiting. Each man slowly began to recover. These men had suffered a near-death experience when an eight-knot following breeze matched the P-100's forward speed. A cloud of carbon monoxide gas had packed into the crew's quarters through open ports, poisoning them. The experience proved to me that a higher power had been watching over us.

We faced other, more benign obstacles as well. New Orleans is the ultimate party town, which made it challenging to maintain discipline among the crew. Four shore patrolmen helped rein in my charges, including conducting bed checks. While it helped that the military made the French Quarter off-limits, this restriction didn't prevent my permanent crew from celebrating every rumor that we were shipping out. The first was in July, and another came in late August when I received tentative orders to sail the P-100 to Brazil—and from there be towed to the Mediterranean, via the Canary Islands, for salvage and rescue duty.

Plans changed, and we were thrilled not to be taking the twenty-five-year-old, under-designed, rough-handling old vessel across the Atlantic.

It was seaworthy enough for Lake Pontchartrain and the Gulf Coast, but not the Atlantic or Mediterranean. By then, the crew and I were ready to ship out, leaving the training to others.

After beginning our assignments at the training school, Andrew Jackson Higgins invited boat skippers to lunch at the St. Charles Hotel in New Orleans. Stories about how he created his company "on a shoestring" were legend. In person, we found him to be friendly, courteous, and a terrific salesman. His record in setting up Higgins Boat Company proved him to be a gutsy, colorful, and exemplary entrepreneur.

In early 1942, after the war started, he realized the US Navy needed builders to construct small wooden-hulled craft, such as landing barges and patrol boats. Approaching local authorities in New Orleans, he reached an agreement to close off two streets in the city's industrial section to set up a construction site. Then he went to the US Navy procurement office in Washington. With only a plan and good salesmanship, Higgins secured an initial contract for $3 million to build motor torpedo boats (MTBs) and small landing craft. He started from scratch, without designers, boat builders, electricians, or small-engine mechanics. There was no shipyard, materials, or a place to store them, only two empty city streets.

New Orleans had a boat-building history, so Andy Higgins gathered available boat builders from along the Gulf Coast and leased old, empty industrial buildings along the canals to shelter them. Higgins Industries constructed more than 20,000 boats during the war. These included swift PT boats for the US, Great Britain, and the Netherlands, twenty-seven-foot airborne lifeboats, and landing craft.

The company designed the landing craft vehicle personnel (LCVP) that played a crucial role during the Normandy invasion on D-Day, June 6, 1944. Through the sheer force of his personality, Higgins performed miracles featuring exceptional American know-how.

The St. Charles Hotel, where we met for lunch, was the pinnacle of gracious living. As we entered the lobby, the American south wrapped us in its warm, friendly traditions. I'll always remember that luncheon because I had been on military rations. Higgins planned it that way because he wanted us to work for him testing PT boats.

Clearing it with our squadron commander, we were permitted to work during our off-duty hours. Smartly, Higgins had set up the Higgins Boat Operators and Marine Engine Maintenance School, realizing that he would have trained helmsmen to test his boats for approval by the Navy.

Our job was to put "slow time" on each PT's three Packard engines, cruising at or near eight knots around Lake Pontchartrain at low rpms. The PTs lacked superstructures, and were controlled by throttles, shifting solenoids, and tachometers. We often docked at Slidell or Madisonville to sample the savory local food as we went around the lake.

Higgins paid us well. And I needed the extra income because my crew was flat broke from partying and didn't have another payday coming for at least a month. So I was the banker. On October 11, we received transfer orders to crew a new sixty-three-foot air-sea rescue boat (AVR 63) under construction at the Fellows & Stewart boatyard in Wilmington, California. Loaded with IOUs, I underwrote our final farewell party.

Our first mission was to shake down the P-399, which was about to be launched for acceptance by the Navy. A sister AVR 63, the P-400, which had been built by Miami Shipbuilding, was commanded by Warrant Officer Marv Pelser and was also ready for testing at Wilmington.

So we bid farewell to New Orleans, bound for California by rail.

2

Wilmington

LANDING IN SUNNY CALIFORNIA, WE LEARNED THAT THE P-399 HAD been christened on July 6, 1943, by Miss Ellen Malcon of Augusta, Kansas, at the Fellows & Stewart boatyard on Pier 206 on Terminal Island in San Pedro. Ellen represented the people of Augusta whose War Bond contributions financed the boat.

Two weeks after our arrival, the P-399 slid down the ways, and I discovered that a man could fall in love at first sight with an inanimate object. A man can have this feeling for his car, a house, or a plane, but it goes deeper for his boat.

The P-399 had graceful lines, a beautiful V-bottom hull double planked with cedar and mahogany, a flying bridge, adequate quarters, a galley, heads, and a sickbay, with a raised cabin just forward of the aft cockpit where we often took our meals. Later, when we were in the South Pacific, we fashioned canvas awnings supported by pipe frames over the flying bridge and aft cockpit to protect us from the searing tropical sun.

It had two powerful twelve-cylinder Hall-Scott "Defender" marine engines, each rated at 630 horsepower at 2100 rpms, which would make it dance over the seas at more than forty knots. When it stepped up on plane, it ran like a scared deer. It was intended for offshore, long-range operations, and designed for high speeds under severe weather conditions.

Although our primary mission was to rescue downed pilots, the P-399 was armed with two twin-mount, .50-caliber machine guns, one on either side of the cockpit. Sometimes a gun would be moved to the foredeck. The boat also carried a single .50-caliber mount in the aft cockpit. Once we reached the war zone, we added a 20-mm gun, salvaged from a downed aircraft, which could be mounted on the foredeck, if necessary.

After the old P-100 in New Orleans, the P-399 was a refreshing change for the crew. They immediately took to her—scrubbing, cleaning, shining, polishing, oiling, and coiling lines—and were eager for shakedown cruises.

Each morning at 0730 hours, we cleared Wilmington Harbor's south or east sea-gates on test runs, conducting gunnery practice, compensating our compasses, and carrying out speed trials (including over the bottom at various engine rpms). We also dropped depth charges (after Navy clearance to ensure one of our subs was not down there) and communicated with signal flags and our radio. The boat passed each test with flying colors.

One evening, when we tied up, there was a message waiting for me from harbor operations, requesting a favor. Would the P-399 provide a ride to Catalina Island for a USO troop performing at the Navy hospital, drop them off, and pick them up at Avalon later in the day? We were, of course, pleased to assist.

The next morning, we were standing by at our dock when two cars arrived at about 1000 hours. One carried George Murphy, the movie star and later US Senator from California, who was the group's leader. With him were film actor Phil Silvers, carrying a clarinet; singer and film actress Deanna Durbin; dancer Patty Thomas; guitarist Tony Romano; and comedian Jerry Colona.

These were generous people, giving their time, sharing their talents, and cheering up those confined in the hospital. The crew had a delightful time with them. Murphy invited us to join them, but we were scheduled to meet target ships and had to decline. At 1800 hours, we picked them up and returned them to shore.

Murphy was enthralled by the P-399, so a couple of days later, we picked him up at Redondo Beach and took him for a run in the Pacific.

Afterward he sometimes arranged for a few of his friends to entertain the P-399 and P-400 crews at their homes or, more often, at fancy restaurants and nightclubs like the Coconut Grove. On these occasions Marv Pelser and I stood watch over our boats. The problem was getting our crews to work the next day.

As a result of Murphy's pals' generosity, I recovered my New Orleans loans, with interest. Wilson Hollis, our radioman, came to me one day, ready to pay up.

"Skip, remember I borrowed some money in New Orleans?" he asked. "How much was it? I want to pay you back."

Since arriving in California we hadn't had a payday, so I was surprised. He pulled out a roll of bills and started to peel off twenties. I got out my little book and told him he had borrowed fifty dollars. He gave me two twenties and a ten. Speechless, I asked whether this was "good money," not stolen, gambled, or from selling his radio equipment.

"Skip, these ladies want to be seen with a serviceman at dinner, so they give me a roll of money to pay for the check. But someone always comes by, or her husband joins us, and they pay the check. They wouldn't take the money back."

During the next two weeks, I recovered all of my loans, plus voluntary interest, from the crew. It was little wonder that I had a hell of a time getting them to leave Hollywood when we were assigned to our next station up the coast in San Francisco.

By early 1944, as deployment to the Southwest Pacific loomed, I decided to fine-tune the crew. It started when I learned that the mate, Warrant Officer Robert Lloyd, was over age in grade and probably wouldn't stand up to the rigors of the pounding we took aboard the P-399, even in light seas.

Warrant Officer (junior grade) Adam Taylor and his oiler, Hal Marshall, were more mechanics than sailors. Our gunner's mate-cook had received two warnings for missing the P-399's early morning departure time, so I classed him as unreliable. Everything depended on men who trusted each other and could work closely together, motivated by the work ahead. I requested permission to recruit replacements. It was a calculated risk, but, fortunately, had excellent results.

The search found our new mate, Master Sergeant George L. Jepson—soon to be known as simply "Jep"—from Marquette, Michigan, on Lake Superior. He had been stationed with the 1004th Quartermaster Boat Company, an AAF air-sea rescue unit at Port O'Connor, Texas. Licensed to "operate and navigate motorboats carrying passengers for hire" by the US Department of Commerce, Jep was qualified to command a crash boat.

On the day Jep's new orders reached his current command, he was aboard a crash boat in the Gulf of Mexico. His headquarters sent an auxiliary craft to collect him. Within hours, he was aboard a plane headed for California, unable, for security reasons, to notify his wife Joyce who worked as a nurse at the local hospital in Victoria. She learned of his departure from a neighbor who worked at the base. They didn't see each other again until after the war ended.

Jep was personable, confident, and quiet, a pipe smoker often wearing a faded green baseball cap. As mate, he rated the rank of warrant officer, junior grade. Reporting aboard in early February, he immediately set about organizing the crew's work, kept the P-399 shipshape, and planned training during the boat's shakedown. In short order, the crew performed their duties better than at any time in the past. As a seasoned sailor, he was the most valuable addition to the P-399.

George Savard, chief engineer, and Bill (Whitey) Chaney, the oiler-gunner, replaced Taylor and Marshall, who were grateful to return to dry land. Savard was an exceptional marine engineer, who babied the P-399's twin Hall-Scott engines, squeezing more rpms out of them. A French Canadian from New Haven, Connecticut, he had served a hitch in the Navy before the war and was stationed at Pearl Harbor. Later he worked there as a civilian and married a dancer at the Royal Hawaiian Hotel and lived the beautiful life in Honolulu.

In early December 1941, Savard and his wife booked passage to the mainland to visit his family in Connecticut. They were at sea aboard the

Matson Line's SS *Lurline*, bound for San Francisco, when the Japanese attacked Pearl Harbor. Naturally worried about their family in Hawaii, the couple wanted to return to the islands. In New Haven, George desperately sought permission to return to Hawaii.

Finally, he learned that the sole solution was to reenlist in the Navy and request assignment to Pearl Harbor. Somehow, he ended up in crash boats, eventually assigned to the P-399 as a warrant officer in charge of the engine room. Based on the Navy's promise, George believed we would end up in the Hawaiian Islands. I didn't tell him about the air-sea rescue units already stationed there.

George chose Bill Chaney from Los Angeles to be his oiler. The pair worked closely together on the engines. Chaney, whom we nicknamed "Whitey," also trained in the care, cleaning, loading, and firing of our twin .50-caliber machine guns.

Ron Albrecht from Milwaukee, Wisconsin, agreed to be our cook—he was surprisingly good at it, too—and gunner's mate. Wilson Hollis, from Bessemer City, North Carolina, stayed aboard as our radio operator and signalman. Danny Tholenaars was our quartermaster. Homer Baker, a native of Cumberland, Maryland, continued as our medical technician and gunner.

Salty, our final crew member, was a brown-and-white terrier puppy, smuggled aboard by Jep, Homer, and Ron. My initial reaction was to put him ashore, but the little guy's friendly tail wagging and facial licks quickly won me over. The pup was a positive influence on the crew and helped bond us into a solid unit. Everyone took great care with Salty, training him for shipboard life. He only barked when George started up the Hall-Scotts in the early morning, and when we were test firing or having target practice with the twin turret .50-caliber machine guns. At night, the little fellow slept at the foot of Jep's bunk.

The crew formed in Wilmington stuck together over the many miles of Pacific Ocean in fair weather and foul.

It was the spring of 1944 and we were ready to ship out, but our destination remained a mystery. In the meantime, only a couple of trials for the boat and crew remained. Luckily, we were able to complete them before we received our shipping orders.

Learning to navigate in the fog occurred unexpectedly. George had shut down the engines to work on them, delaying our return to base after an offshore run. As we approached to within four miles of the north entrance to the harbor, heavy fog forced us to reduce our speed to a crawl. We felt our way in, assisted by the port foghorn, a bell buoy, and, once in a great while, a break in the fog allowing me to pick up lights on Point Fermin.

At last, after what seemed like forty miles instead of four, I picked up the north entrance visually. Inside the breakwater, there were enough lights to navigate and we finally docked the P-399, happy to tie up. That soup provided valuable experience.

Our next trial "blooded" the P-399 and crew. Weather reports warned of a near-hurricane-force line storm with sixty-mile-per-hour winds that was predicted to hit the Wilmington area during the night. Hollis picked up an announcement on our base radio that small craft would not be permitted to leave the harbor.

I called the crew together and told them we were sailing about twenty miles due south to Balboa, near Newport Beach, to gas up. The southerly course would have the boat broadside to massive waves. I plotted a course, assuming we could get out of the harbor, which would quarter the seas and take advantage of the wind to keep us from sailing too far away from shore and our correct course.

Even though the crew understood the risks involved, there wasn't a glance or murmur from anyone when I ordered all hands on deck. George was strapped to the engine room below; Whitey was to relieve him every thirty minutes.

Jep didn't question whether we could run the south sea-gate with small-craft-warning flags snapping in the wind and guards stationed over the egress. We both knew they would report the P-399 to Navy Operations and the Los Angeles Port of Debarkation Commander. The submarine nets at each of the harbor entrances were three fathoms below mean tide levels, so that wouldn't be a problem; we drew only five and a half feet. So, off we charged.

As we approached the south sea-gate, lookouts waved us off. We acted as though we didn't see them, or the flag warnings. Inside the Wilmington breakwater the waves were high, but nothing like the seas that hit us as we cleared the gate. The guards screamed, unheeded, into the wind. We plunged into the teeth of a full gale. Sailing the P-399, setting the proper speed, and quartering the huge waves left little time to consider the prudence of running in the storm, but it was essential to prepare us for what might lie ahead.

Green water crashed and streamed over the deck. The biting spray, blown by the hurricane-like winds, made it impossible to talk. We communicated by hand signs and shouting. The boat lurched and shuddered as towering waves hit us broadside. There was not a creak or a groan from the hull.

I steered to quarter the crashing seas, and the P-399 rode up one side, listed to starboard, righted herself in the trough, and climbed the next monstrous wave. The crew had battened down all ports and companionway hatches. Even though the decks were awash, we weren't taking on excessive water. Our bilge pumps were working well. The crew—including Salty—wore kapok life vests. They hung onto the bridge structure, standing by to inflate our eight-man life raft if necessary, repeating earlier deck drills.

The engines ran at low rpms. I judged that we were making about four knots, with the wind keeping us near the shore. Even with the poor visibility, Jep sighted a water tower near the shoreline, allowing us to get our bearings. As we struggled to cover each mile, waves cascaded over the deck, but the P-399 handled them like a true thoroughbred.

For a brief time visibility improved, and we could see the breakwater entrance to Newport Beach and Balboa. We had traveled nineteen nautical miles at an estimated speed of four knots supported by calculations based on sighting objects on shore.

At the next break in the waves, I decided to turn the boat to an easterly course toward the entrance. A sailor's myth is that every fourth wave is the largest. As I brought the helm around, steering us into the still-huge waves, we encountered a significant groundswell. The waves picked us up and thrust us toward the shore, with no steering control. I remembered a lesson learned piloting the old P-100 in New Orleans that indicated that in a following sea, your boat will broach and you will have no control unless you outrun the waves.

So we increased our speed and aimed for the harbor entrance, crashing up against one side of a wave, breaking through, and sliding down the leeward side, and then up the next. We were taking a beating but the boat didn't broach badly, and we maintained steerage while I changed course twice to align with the opening.

As we closed on the entrance, it looked very narrow. But the decision had been made and could not be reversed. Again, I increased speed and yelled to the crew, "Here we go!" Once inside the breakwater, I throttled back, reducing speed, and we slipped into what felt like a calm millpond. Even the wind seemed less gusty. How the P-399 hit the center of the entrance, I'll never know. I believe it was prayers, dumb luck, and the seaworthy boat and crew.

We found our way to the gas dock and the pumps with 100-plus octane aviation fuel. The operator greeted us as though we had come through a light breeze. "Glad to see you," he said. "I haven't had many customers today." He didn't mention a word about our being insane to challenge this storm.

After receiving permission to tie up at the end of the dock, all hands, except for Whitey and me, went ashore. We filled our tanks, which took considerable time because we had to strain the fuel through a chamois. Later, Whitey and I also went ashore for food and a well-deserved beer.

It was good to be dry again. Speaking by radio with Wilmington Harbor Operations, I explained why we had run the south sea-gate. A voice on the other end mentioned that a complaint had been lodged, but I never heard from them.

The next day each man in the crew let me know they hadn't been sure about challenging the storm but were now confident that we could sail the P-399 anywhere under any weather conditions. This confidence was to be tested again and again in the months ahead. We were storm "blooded." Importantly, the crew accepted me as their skipper.

When we returned to Wilmington Harbor, waving to the sea-gate keepers as we passed through, I was satisfied that we were as ready as we would ever be to meet whatever might lie ahead.

A few days later orders arrived telling us to proceed to San Francisco, our port of embarkation for the Southwest Pacific.

3

San Francisco

On February 24, the P-399 and P-400 were deck-loaded aboard a Liberty ship, and we steamed north to San Francisco, the magical city on the bay where singer Tony Bennett has since left his heart. The city's maritime history stretches back to the earliest days of exploration along California's coast, and it played a significant role in the development of the American West.

We would have liked to sail the P-399 under the Golden Gate Bridge and along the historic shoreline—the Embarcadero, Fort Mason, the wharves that greeted sailing ships bringing families, news, and prospectors seeking gold around Cape Horn. Instead, we soaked up the scenes around the bay from the Liberty's deck.

After off-loading the boat, our appreciation for the local history heightened as we tied up at a yacht marina on the bay near the Presidio, which lies almost in the shadow of the Golden Gate Bridge. Other than Whitey, whose home was in California, none of us had ever seen this part of the country.

Preparations for shipping us to the war zone were now getting serious. There was no time for cruising around Treasure Island, Alcatraz, Oakland, or even Coyote Point. Our orders were to ready the P-399 and the P-400 for shipping to an unknown destination.

We painted the boat's hull a light blue that wouldn't silhouette against the sky once we loaded aboard a Liberty that would transport us to the Pacific war zone. There was concern about enemy submarines as we made our way across the Pacific. We coated our armament with cosmoline (a thick combination of grease and oil) and secured our equipment, which included manila line, medical/sickbay supplies, galley supplies (excluding food), a full issue of .50-caliber ammunition, paint, wool blankets, engine room supplies, and other (mostly unauthorized) things.

While checking in at Fort Mason, I was told, off the record, that an officer who was shipping out could buy tax-free whiskey from National Distilleries. I immediately hailed a cab, went over, and bought a case of Three Feathers. I would have liked several cases but only knew where to hide one aboard the boat.

Officially alcoholic beverages were banned aboard ships, except for medicinal purposes. I obtained a box marked "Medical Supplies," packed the case of Three Feathers in it, and carried it aboard. No one in the crew knew what was in the box. Once in my quarters, I lifted the deck boards, put padding between the ribs and the hull, and secured the bottles with heavy waterproof tape. Despite the boat's pounding in monstrous seas, we didn't lose a bottle in the months to come.

After loading the P-399, there was little for us to do but wait for shipping orders. On each day that came with no shipping date, we became tourists.

One afternoon while we were relaxing on the deck, the owner of a beautiful pastel-colored home fronting the bay came down and invited us to dinner. It was a swell evening with a warm and friendly family whose son was in the service. During our remaining time in San Francisco, several families along the Embarcadero invited us for picnics and cookouts.

According to some of the crew, San Francisco had inviting nightlife. The hotels all had clubs—one near Union Square was nicknamed the Snakepit—with top-notch entertainment. Every meal we ate was special because we knew it could be our last in the US for a while. These repasts remained in our memories for months to come.

Marv Pelser and I did 'Frisco together: Fisherman's Wharf, Chinatown (twice), and the Top of the Mark (breathtaking). The Presidio, Oakland, and Sausalito were also delightful to visit. The Fairmont Hotel had opened one of its grand ballrooms and installed cots for servicemen to sleep on without charge. It was packed the night Marv and I were there.

Our orders finally came through in late February. The P-399 and P-400 were deck-loaded aboard the Liberty ship *James J. Corbett*. I couldn't look when the crane lifted the P-399 out of the water, but the operator, a real pro, eased the cradle down onto the deck an inch at a time. I heaved a sigh of relief once it was loaded safely.

Finally the day came for us to wave goodbye to San Francisco, her classy and friendly people, and the Golden Gate Bridge. The *Corbett*'s navigator, who became a good friend during our voyage, said we would pick up destroyer escorts off the Gulf of California, which didn't happen. The farther south we sailed, the more confident we became that a Japanese submarine was stalking us, but if one was out there, it didn't act.

George Savard was still sure we were headed for Hawaii and was bitterly disappointed when we sailed by the islands' latitude. There would be no Hawaii, and no family reunion, and he never trusted the Navy again. The *Corbett* was bound for the Fiji Islands. We could hardly wait to get the P-399 in the water and get to work.

4

Fiji to Guadalcanal

ON THE 4,500-MILE VOYAGE TO THE SOUTH PACIFIC ABOARD THE COR-*bett*, we studied the identification of American and Japanese aircraft and ships. Hollis worked with *Corbett*'s radioman, "Sparks." Ron spent time in the galley, with the ship's cooks, while Baker boned up on his knowledge with the third officer, the ship's medical technician.

Crossing the equator, we attended King Neptune's Court and became Shellbacks, members of the Ancient Order of the Deep. The Navy gun crew conducted the traditional ritual. Every one of us had our heads shaved as part of the initiation. Jep was relieved the court didn't touch the goatee he was nurturing.

During the voyage the captain invited me to the bridge, providing an excellent opportunity to gain additional understanding in navigating the vast South Pacific while working with the second officer. After the evening mess, he and I frequently went on deck and talked navigation. His knowledge of the Polynesians, Melanesians, and Micronesians and how they voyaged the vast reaches of the Pacific was exceptional. Jep also worked on navigational problems.

Ancestors of the Pacific islanders migrated across the South Pacific from the far west to the east, settling the Carolines, Marshalls, Gilberts, Hawaii, French Polynesia, Society, Solomons, Bismarck Archipelago, and many other island groups. They were guided by the sun, moon, stars, wind, tides, and currents.

Like most Americans, I had a vision of the way a tropical island would look. Still, I was not prepared for the exquisite early morning light in the Samoa Islands as we sailed by Pago Pago, one of the smaller islands in the group.

Our destination was Suva, Fiji, with its tall, graceful coconut palm trees and blue-green sea with white, lace-like foam decorating the white-tan sand beaches. Along the shore, outrigger canoes and frond-covered cottages nestled among the palm groves made an idyllic setting. The azure blue sky met the deep blue of the open sea and contrasted the pure green of the hills and mountains on the islands. The splendor challenged my ideas of what makes Earth beautiful.

We hoped to have the P-399 lifted off the *Corbett*'s deck by a large crane at Suva Harbor, where we could clean the boat, engines, and armament; unpack our gear; and prepare for air-sea rescue missions, but there was no barge crane large enough. So, the *Corbett* headed for Espiritu Santo in the New Hebrides group, hoping to unload us there. It was about a 250-nautical-mile voyage through what the Navy designated Japanese submarine hunting grounds.

The first day out we joined a small convoy, three supply ships, and a tanker, escorted by a destroyer and a destroyer escort, also headed for Espiritu Santo.

Sailing into Segond Channel at Santos we observed the reality of war for the first time. Lying on its port side was the troopship *Woodrow Wilson*. It was sunk, not by the Japanese, but by one of our submerged mines. The ship's captain had smartly steered his ship out of the channel so it wouldn't block shipping. It had rolled over on its side and lay partly out of the water. The five thousand troops aboard all survived the mishap.

After the *Corbett* moored, Navy operations officers came aboard to inform us that although a large crane was available, we would remain aboard and continue for another two hundred miles west to Guadalcanal and the Solomon Islands where the Navy MTB base at Tulagi Island, across Sealark Channel from Guadalcanal, had a crane to unload the P-399 and P-400. Also aboard the *Corbett* were two twin-engine P-61

Black Widows for the 13th Air Force's Sixth Night Fighter Squadron based on the island.

Facing a two-day delay at Santos, the crew requested leave to go ashore. They had heard that local islanders would dive off a high tower with their only chance to survive severe injury or death depending on a rope of woven vines tied to their ankles. Bungee jumping just may have originated there. The crew wanted to check it out, but the port officer was not sure when the *Corbett* would depart and denied the request.

Eventually we continued our journey and the *Corbett* entered the southern end of The Slot, or the Sealark Channel, between Guadalcanal, Savo Island, and Florida Island. Arriving at Lunga Point in the wake of the Japanese submarine scare, we were relieved to start our mission after several months of preparing back in California. A crane lifted us off the *Corbett's* deck, and the P-399 and P-400 settled in the lagoon, mooring at Kukum Dock. It was May 1944. The *Sea Horse* would carry us from the Solomons to the Philippines over the next year and a half. VJ-Day was a long way off.

Guadalcanal had been the starting point of the island war against the Japanese. The Battle of Guadalcanal—code-named Operation Watchtower—was fought between August 7, 1942, and February 9, 1943, on the island and the surrounding waters. It was the first major land offensive against the Japanese by the Allied forces. During the battle, nearby Savo Sound became known as Ironbottom Sound in grim recognition of the ships, including four American cruisers, and planes lost between August and November 1942.

We arrived several months after the fierce fighting between US Marines and the Japanese on the island, and the naval battles in the surrounding waters, so we didn't experience the worst days of the war there.

Thick steamy jungle covered most of the island's 2,700-square-mile area. It was more than ninety miles long and thirty-three miles wide. Climbing vines and flowers, including orchids of beautiful shapes and colors, covered massive mahogany, banyan, rosewood, and cypress trees. Tropical plants, many with needle-like barbs edging broad leaves, covered the forest floor.

Weather was oppressive for both crew and boat. Temperatures under the tropical sun climbed over 100°F on most days. Storms with low, scudding clouds and sheets of rain blew through frequently, causing steam to rise from the deck when the sun showed through again. The humidity was unbearable. You could sweat a quart an hour standing still.

The sun beating down on the deck was so hot that it was impossible to go without shoes. Sneakers and moccasins shipped from home were favored footwear. Ashore, we encountered dirt and dust, the stench of rotting jungle foliage, and the threat of mosquito-borne malaria, which almost everyone on board eventually contracted. During our entire time in the Pacific, we slept aboard the boat.

At Guadalcanal, I was appointed commander of the Fifteenth Emergency Rescue Boat Squadron assigned to the 13th AAF, which earned the nickname "The Jungle Air Force." There were four boats with us, including the P-400, P-406, and a 110-footer. The latter served as our supply ship, storing our spare propeller, two drive shafts, and an extra wheel.

Maintaining a wooden boat the size of the P-399 in the tropics was a constant challenge requiring frequent painting and, on one occasion, the replacement of wormy planks near the bow. Dair Long, the boat's designer at Miami Shipbuilding Company, showed great foresight when he conceived a double-planked hull, making it possible for the crew to complete repairs in the war zone with minimal time lost.

Moored at Kukum Dock, we had front-row seats to fighter planes taking off from Henderson Field as they flew right over our mast. As all hands worked to keep the boat in the best operating condition possible, we waited for our orders to join the 13th Air Force fighter-bomber groups that had recently moved north to Munda, New Georgia's airfields. Until those orders came, we were temporarily under 13th Air Force Service Command, a supply unit.

After arriving at Guadalcanal, Jep said the crew wanted to give the P-399 a name. Some suggestions were X-rated. After much arbitration and compromise, the P-399 became the *Sea Horse*, an apt name because that boat was a thoroughbred in the purest sense.

Around this time we also built platforms underneath the dock where we spent time off the boat. We had a diving face mask and air compressor aboard so we took turns salvaging goods accidentally dropped from nets while the Liberty ships were unloading. Among items retrieved were a case of Lifesaver candies, which came in handy when we visited islands, and a case of government issue .45-caliber semiautomatic pistols. Other merchandise included canned goods, toothpaste, shaving cream, and beer.

In the Army you were allowed to drink beer, but we had a rule aboard the boat that we wouldn't drink unless we were off duty. Beer shipments loaded aboard trucks on the dock were stacked as high as possible. As trucks headed down the dock, someone would jump up on the truck bed and knock as many cases as possible into the water. We kept beer in nets submerged in the cool water beneath the platforms. The heat was oppressive, so a nice cold beer or Coke hit the spot.

In the mornings before breakfast and in the evenings after mess, Jep and some of the others swam or fished with gear sent from the States. Although the fishing was rather good, Jep said it didn't compare to the freshwater catches on Lake Superior off Marquette in Michigan's Upper Peninsula, but it provided Cookie (our nickname for Ron Albrecht) with variety for our menu.

Some evenings, unless it was raining, which was a regular occurrence, we'd go to outdoor movies. One night it'd be a cowboy shoot-'em-up and the next a war film like *The Fighting Seabees*. Eating was also a pleasant pastime when we were off patrol. Ron's chocolate-covered donuts kept the crew happy, along with his tasty meals.

Salty was a pleasant diversion for the crew and often served as an alarm clock in the morning, jumping on Jep or barking at movement aboard the *Sea Horse*. At Guadalcanal, mail arrived about three times a week, raising spirits with each passing month we were away from home. Packages containing hard-to-find items like cigars and tobacco were especially appreciated.

Jep confided that Joyce was expecting a baby in the fall and we soon had a wager between us. I bet on a girl and he put his money on a boy, hoping to add a fourth George to the family line of himself, his father, and his grandfather.

Since the Japanese attack on Pearl Harbor, press reports from the Pacific and Europe had been discouraging, but the news from Guadalcanal in the late summer of 1942 made Americans proud.

On August 7, 1942, the First Marine Division's Fifth Regiment had come ashore at Koli Point, about two and a half miles from Lunga Point, and fought their way inland. The Japanese airfield, completed the day before, was given up with only token resistance. Had it not been taken, this strategic installation could have rendered Allied bases at Espiritu Santo and Samoa useless, blocking our supply shipping lanes to the west.

Colonel Merritt Edson's First Raider Battalion occupied a ridge on the south side of what American forces named Henderson Field, giving his fighters an advantage. The Japanese launched their most massive attacks with banzai charges and finally broke through the Marine positions, allowing them to reach the edge of the airstrip. Just as it was needed most, a strange mix of Marines from supply units—laundry, communications, weapons, ordnance, and even the marine band, all attached to the Second Battalion, Seventh Marines—joined the battle. Hand-to-hand fighting helped drive the enemy from what became known as Bloody Ridge.

The next morning, before the Japanese could regroup and add fresh troops, AAF fighters flew in at palm-tree level and strafed them with streams of .50-caliber machine gun and 20-mm cannon fire, disorganizing enemy ranks and saving the airfield.

Once secured, the airstrip became Henderson Field to honor Marine Corps Major Lofton Henderson, commanding officer of Marine Scout Bombing Squadron 241 (VMSB-241) during the Battle of Midway. Leading his squadron against the Japanese carrier forces, Henderson became the first Marine aviator lost during the battle.

The area west of Henderson Field, toward Cape Esperance, was occupied by entrenched Japanese and became a living jungle hell. Our Marines had to dig them out of camouflaged holes along the rivers.

On the eastern end of Guadalcanal, there are two extinct volcano peaks covered halfway up their sides with jungle growth. The tree canopy was so dense that the sun could not penetrate through the leaves on the brightest day. You had to cut your way through the vines, barbed palmettos, and reeds with a machete. The bush swarmed with flies, other bugs, and malarial mosquitoes. Stepping into this humid hell, your clothing became sweat-soaked in minutes.

The fighter and bomber squadrons flying out of Henderson Field became famous for their skills and courage. First, it was the Sixty-Seventh Fighter Squadron, which later became part of the 13th Air Force. Their tireless ground crews kept a few old wrecks patched up and flying. At that time, new planes mostly went to Europe.

Everyone at Guadalcanal was exhausted most of the time. The Japanese sent bombing raids down the Slot several times each night. Their light Betty bombers were nicknamed "Washing Machine Charlie" (because of their engines' high whine) and "Piss Call Charlie" (which is self-explanatory). Our pilots respected Japan's ace, nicknamed "Pistol Pete," who flew his nimble, quick-performing Zero against our slower P-40s.

Later, when we received the twin-tailed P-38 Lightning fighters, our pilots outflew, outmaneuvered, and chased the Japanese back to their home base, totally beaten. In the meantime, Pistol Pete dropped light bombs on Henderson Field with deadly accuracy. Marine fighter pilot Pappy Boyington and his Black Sheep Squadron became legends as they fearlessly and aggressively flew their gull-winged F4U Corsairs up and down the Slot.

A story made the rounds about four Black Sheep pilots who were playing bridge in the ready room when the radio crackled and a voice announced that six Japanese planes were Guadalcanal-bound. One of the Black Sheep pilots got up, put on his Mae West, and calmly said, "I'll go . . . I'm dummy this hand."

New Zealand and Australian air forces also used the airstrips at Henderson Field and nearby Kukum Field to train new pilots to fly the F4U

Corsair, a pretty hot plane. It was inevitable that some wouldn't get airborne, due to pilot error, and, we learned, a poor air-petrol carburetor mix. When one splashed down in Lunga Lagoon, about fifty yards offshore, we made our first rescue aboard the *Sea Horse* without even starting our engines.

Jep and Whitey went overboard, swam to the Anzac aircraft, rescued the pilot, and, with the help of the *Sea Horse*, secured a line on the tail and pulled it close to the beach. Their actions earned commendations from the New Zealand Air Force.

Our first "off-duty" mission was to patrol off Florida, Malaita, Tulagi, and Santa Isabel. It felt great to have the sea under us. But the full realization that we were at war, even more than seeing the Washing Machine Charlies, struck us as we returned to base.

Usually, if an aircraft was down, we received coordinates from the tower to help us locate the pilot. The coordinates fell within a square grid with numbers down one side and names down another. By connecting a name, say "Amy," we could determine where to look with a number. The names were changed daily to prevent the Japanese from picking up the location while monitoring our radio traffic.

Pilots had a green dye packet on their Mae Wests, which they released to assist us and aircraft in spotting them. We also looked for oil slicks in the area of a crash. Most of the time, we had air cover to protect us on a rescue mission.

On this occasion we received a report that an American fighter had gone down in the channel over toward Tulagi. When we arrived in the general area we did a thorough search and eventually found an oil slick, but were unable to find the aircraft or the pilot. Two P-38 fighters from the squadron that had lost the plane provided air cover and eyes from the sky. On the way back to Guadalcanal, the P-38s decided to give us a friendly buzz, diving on either side of the boat.

The first fighter pulled out of its dive at about five hundred feet. The second pilot misjudged his altitude, a common mistake over water, and plunged nose-first into the sea off our starboard bow. The plane hit the water close enough to splash our deck. We immediately stopped.

Jep and another crewman went overboard and swam to the pilot, floating face down, still strapped to his seat. The plane had simply disintegrated. They turned him over and got him to the side of the boat, where we lowered a wire basket. Sadly, he didn't survive. The other pilot continued back to base, unaware that his wingman had crashed.

Seeing this young man's life snuffed out instantly shocked each of us to the core. This useless loss was imprinted on our souls and memories forever. I wrote to his parents, describing what had happened. The pages of that note were stained with my tears for their tragic loss. Nearly fifty years later, Jep related the story to his oldest son, George, and broke down recalling this vivid memory.

Another day, a New Zealand Corsair crashed into the sea on takeoff from nearby Kukum Field (also known as Fighter II Strip). The P-406, commanded by Warrant Officer John Cranston, responded immediately and picked up the pilot. Jep and Warrant Officer Paul Roberts from Cranston's crew volunteered to dive on the submerged aircraft to determine what position the plane's controls were in and retrieve the instrument readings for New Zealand's investigation of the crash. Both received commendations from the New Zealand Air Force.

Our time at Guadalcanal also had relatively quiet periods. Off patrol, we worked on the boat, painting it inside and out and keeping it shipshape in general. When we discovered shipworms had invaded planks near the bow, we moved into a Navy drydock where ship carpenters replaced the damaged wood. At the same time we camouflaged the hull, spray painting it with three shades of green. To protect the pilot house, we replaced the window glass with aluminum sheeting. Another time, we exchanged our kerosene stove for an electric unit taken from a wrecked bomber.

Much of my time off patrol was spent in the pilothouse digging out from under piles of paperwork or onshore dealing with the military bureaucracy. I continued to report our readiness for duty to headquarters as we waited for our orders to join the 13th Air Force fighting units farther. No word arrived, and we waited and waited, not so patiently, patrolling Ironbottom Sound while the war moved up the Slot.

It didn't take long for malaria to strike the crew. Near the end of July the mosquito-borne disease hit Jep, who was hospitalized for more than a week. Each morning, the crew made the trek to the infirmary to visit him and deliver mail. I usually waited to visit until evening. It wasn't long before everyone aboard the *Sea Horse* had malaria with varying levels of discomfort. As we recovered and Jep was able to return to the boat, Salty was excited to see him.

One day we received an order to sail to coded grid coordinates and cover an aircraft with a VIP aboard on a flight line from Australia. We were to remain there until given an "all clear." Operations only said the plane was a Douglas C-54. They didn't identify the VIP. We returned to base at Lunga Point the next day, without even seeing the aircraft.

On my birthday, July 5, we had a nice steak dinner and a little gathering afterward with a couple of other crash boat skippers and some of their crews. All together we consumed three quarts of whiskey and a few beers. An enjoyable time was had by all—until the next morning when we were laid low with screaming hangovers.

On August 7 we attended a USO show headlined by Bob Hope, Francis Langford, and Jerry Colonna. We had great seats about thirty feet from the stage. A western feature film followed the hour-and-a-half stage performance. Later that month, Jack Benny arrived on Guadalcanal with Martha Tilton, best known for her 1939 recording of "And the Angels Sing" with Benny Goodman. It was a terrific show. Despite the pleasant distractions, we all were anxious to move closer to the 13th Air Force operations farther up the Slot.

Bad luck struck with a little warning one morning as we prepared to go out on patrol. The weather had been ideal up until then, but that morning I noticed the islanders had pulled their fishing boats well up onto the beach instead of going out to fish on the reef. Women were heading up a trail leading inland with their heads stacked high with their possessions. I asked Hollis for another weather report from Navy operations. The forecast was for a calm, tropical day, with a chance of a line storm.

The lagoon was like a millpond, no sign of a breeze. There were no birds over the offshore fishing area. I asked Baker to go over to the small village and speak to the islanders. They spoke a mixture of Australian English and a made-up language taught to them by missionaries. Bake did as I asked and returned saying the islanders predicted that a massive storm would hit Guadalcanal in a few hours.

I walked over to the P-400 and told Marv Pelser, who had received orders to transfer his boat to the Russell Islands in two days. Marv had also heard the favorable weather report but decided to sail with us to the south end of the island and seek protection. Neither of us could take the chance of having our boats stacked up on the beach.

I set a course around Cape Esperance, on the western end of Guadal-canal, where we could hopefully find a sheltered cove to offer protection from high winds and crashing seas. Sure enough, less than an hour after reporting our decision to tower operations, a light breeze started blowing and the sea became choppy. The wind increased steadily.

By the time we found a small cove on the lee side of the island, set a stern anchor, and secured heavy lines to stumps and trees near the shore, a "bloody gile," as the Aussies called them, was blowing full force. Palm trees bent and dry fronds sailed over our heads. A hill offered some protection but the storm tossed us about and strained the boat's lines. Through it all, the P-399 weathered the storm with no problems.

By early afternoon the winds increased, blowing palms over, send-ing their coconuts rolling into the waves that were crashing and foaming over the narrow beach. We could only imagine how rough it was on the windward side of the island.

The eye of the storm passed over and the backside winds, which were not as strong, gradually decreased in force. The seas continued to pound the shore but had calmed enough the next morning for us to take in our lines and start back to Lunga.

The *Sea Horse* was riding the waves well when we suddenly lost steerage. The force of the storm, and possibly earlier heavy weather, had cracked and loosened the bronze rudder casting. Anticipating such an event, Fellows & Stewart had provided a manual rudder, stored in the stern lazaret.

Jep and George rigged the back-up rudder while we were broadside to the sea, which was no easy task. After half an hour, they had it working and I moved from the bridge to steer with the stern auxiliary tiller. Bake and Ron stood at the bridge compass, signaling the course line to me. The jury-rig worked and we made it back to Lunga Lagoon. Our wharf and metal drum float were a shamble after being washed ashore during the storm, along with several island vessels.

Operations gave us a "four-oh" when we reported after anchoring. At the next high tide, we backed our stern into the shallow water. At low tide, with the propellers off the sandy bottom, George and Whitey removed the cracked rudder casting and took it to the Navy Seabees to have it machined and brazed. Two days later we were back in business.

On July 12, 1944, while we were still waiting for sailing orders, Henderson Field operations notified us that a C-47 hospital plane had crashed into the side of Marau Peak, which had been formed by a volcano on the east end of the island. Aboard were a three-man crew and four passengers who had just been released from the base hospital in Nandi, Fiji, and were returning to active duty.

Search planes, responding to a mayday call, spotted the crash site. We stood by, waiting for a doctor from our station hospital to join us for a land rescue, which while part of our job was the least practiced. The *Sea Horse,* along with the P-613, sped along the coast to Markina (number one), a village near the base of the peak. Ron and George stayed aboard on watch while the rest of us took two folding litters, K rations, and medical supplies and went ashore.

As fortune would have it, there was a Jesuit priest in the small village. He organized a rescue squad of four villagers who joined the doctor and our crew on the long, tedious, and tiring climb. The trail wound upward through the jungle, over rocks, and across rushing whitewater streams.

Even though I was in decent shape, the doctor and I struggled to keep up with the islanders and our younger crew. The group politely paused often to allow us to catch up.

It was late afternoon when we reached Markina Village (number two) on the volcano's tree-covered side, still some distance from where locals said the plane had crashed. They had found one survivor and had made a leafy bed for him. The doctor, Baker, and Whitey went with our guides to the wreck. Bodies were removed and arranged for burial until Graves Registration could rebury them in Henderson Field Cemetery. The lone survivor, a young Marine corporal, was placed in a litter and was attended to all night by the doctor, with Baker periodically relieving him.

We had given some of our K rations to the village volunteers and had little left for an evening meal. The upper village leader motioned that he wanted us to share their food, which was turning on a spit over an open fire near his grass shack.

The priest from Markina (number one) told me that these Melanesian islanders were safe, explaining that the government had imposed severe punishment for cannibalism—or eating "long pig"—over the last several years. As a result, the ceremonial custom had ceased. In earlier years, warriors had been known to attack a village, steal their women, and take a prisoner back to their own village to be cooked and eaten in a tribal ceremony.

This knowledge didn't help my appetite in the least. Our guides and some villagers were cooking something as black as charcoal on a spit. We each received a hunk of meat. I felt the eyes of the crew watching me, wondering what I would do. To maintain friendly relations with our hosts, who also might have been watching me, I took a big bite. Aside from the burnt taste, it wasn't bad washed down with coconut milk. The crew ate, too. Later, we learned that the meat was dove.

When we returned to the P-399 with the injured Marine, I was grateful that land rescues and mountain climbing were rare occurrences. An ambulance was waiting for us at our dock, rebuilt after the storm. The doctor and his patient, who was still in some shock but doing well, left for the field hospital at Henderson.

It was quiet aboard the *Sea Horse* as we absorbed the sad reality of the C-47 crewmen and the passengers who had lost their lives. There was no music that evening.

Orders still had not come for us to join the fighting units at Munda, New Georgia, so we continued to patrol around Guadalcanal, Malaita, Savo, Florida, Tulagi, and Santa Isabel—almost to the southern end of the Slot.

History happened here, on the land, in the air, and in Ironbottom Sound's sacred waters. It was a legacy left by those who came before us that we never forgot. At Tassafaronga Point, across the channel between Savo Island and Guadalcanal, monuments stand in tribute to America's victory, won at a tremendous cost in lives and ships.

A lighter story about Savo Island involved a species of small birds using volcanic beaches to hatch their young. According to the tale, female birds laid their eggs in the warm sand and when they hatched, the young would come out of their shells and fly away.

After one patrol we were met at our dock by a captain and his aide from the commander's office of the AAF Service Command. I stepped onto the dock and received a verbal order to have the P-399 at Boko-kimbo Beach near Service Command Headquarters at 0800 hours the following day to pick up a small party. There were no further details.

The next morning we stood offshore as ordered and received a signal to pick up passengers. The crew put our small eight-foot dinghy overboard and Baker rowed it to shore. It took four trips to bring aboard two majors, a captain, a lieutenant, three nurses, picnic boxes, a traveling bar, and three fishing rods and gear.

One of the majors directed us to take them to a "good fishing spot" on the Sealark Channel. I turned blue along with crew members close to the bridge when we heard the demand. I couldn't refuse to obey a direct order, so we headed for the fishing grounds. Several hours later, the lady passengers and one officer weren't feeling well, so we unloaded the party at Taivu Beach.

On the sail back to Lunga, I expressed to the crew my opposition to using the *Sea Horse* for entertaining and promised to renew my efforts to secure orders to join the 13th Air Force units at Munda, New Georgia.

Two days later I received an order from the commanding general of the Service Command to pick up passengers at the beach near Boko-kimbo. I nearly had a mutiny on my hands when I told the crew, but we couldn't refuse a direct order, especially from a brigadier general.

The next day the general, some of his staff officers, and station nurses came aboard. Two officers brought along fishing gear and requested that I take the P-399 through shallow coral reefs. I refused, which prompted the general to visit the bridge, directing me to take the boat closer to shore. I respectfully told him the P-399 was my responsibility and that I would not knowingly damage it unless to save a life, adding that if he put the order in writing I would obey it. He stomped away down the deck with undisguised anger, obviously not used to first lieutenants refusing to act on his orders.

George and I met below and arranged for an engine to "break down." George shut the Hall-Scotts down and I let the *Sea Horse* ride sideways to the three-foot waves, wallowing in the trough with a lazy, rocking motion. It didn't take long before one of the nurses was sick over the side.

A major went into the engine room to hurry George's "repairs" along and demanded that he start the engines. About half an hour later, George turned over the starboard engine, and the general, who was becoming pale under his tan, requested we return the party to the island.

George started the "fixed" port engine and we lost no time conveying our passengers back to the beach.

Baker exacted a bit of revenge when he directed the general to our din-ghy's aft seat to row him to shore. The P-399's hull had six-inch exhausts on each side, with hot water flowing out of them from the engines. Bake "accidentally" backed the general's backside right up to an exhaust outlet.

Aboard the *Sea Horse* that evening and the next day there was an unusual silence. The lack of usual banter continued for the next few days. I ate alone in my quarters until Jep and George asked me to come to the stern cockpit. Jep said the crew didn't blame me for the party trips but was anxious to move up to the combat zone.

A few days later, while we were patrolling near Savo Island, the air was shattered with explosion after explosion on Guadalcanal. Jep estimated that the blasts were coming from near Henderson Field. We had been on air alert, so we knew there had not been a bombing attack.

After returning to the dock we learned that the explosions occurred at the ordnance supply dump near the airstrip, set off by fire spreading through kunai grass growing over the whole area.

It turned out that a corporal walking guard duty wanted one of the small parachutes attached to flares. As the flare shot into the sky, it released a small parachute that slowed the flare's descent back to the ground and allowed the attached burning magnesium to light night skies. So the corporal fired a flare, and when it hit the ground, it ignited the kunai grass.

Up went an estimated $75 million in ordnance, including bombs and big-gun shells for battlewagons. The corporal didn't get his expensive parachute. According to reports, the loss delayed the invasion of Tawara.

Each day we expected orders to move up to Munda, where the 13th Air Force was fighting an all-out war against Japanese bases on Bougainville and New Britain. We believed the *Sea Horse* would be an asset rescuing downed flyers.

5

Personal Bomb

RETURNING FROM A ROUTINE PATROL ONE AFTERNOON, WE FOUND AN AAF captain and a master sergeant, both wearing MP bands, waiting for us in a jeep on the pier at Lunga Point when the *Sea Horse* docked. The captain ordered me to turn command over to the next ranking officer, in this case, George, a warrant officer, and accompany them to headquarters.

Astonished, I directed George and Jep, responsible for the deck when I wasn't aboard, to work together until I returned. They wanted to know what was happening, but I couldn't tell them anything. The best I could do was remain calm while I was taken away.

The jeep sped off, leaving the P-399 in its wake, heading over fifteen miles on a Pacific island road, a quagmire of mud and gray slush in the morning and after a rainstorm. On most days, this road turned into a dust rut that billowed with traffic, irritating the lungs of those traveling in vehicles. It was a long, silent ride. Despite my queries, the captain offered no explanations.

After what seemed like a couple of hours, we arrived at headquarters in the early evening. Under an armed guard, I spent the night in a screened Dale Hut, without dinner, only learning that the general from our recent fishing excursion would see me in the morning. During a mostly sleepless night, I went over the fishing trip in my mind, wondering what might have caused the general to do this. I couldn't believe the turn of events.

Early the next morning, after breakfasting on lukewarm coffee and stale toast, I was taken, without a shave or shower, to the general's office, where I stood at attention. Several officers from the fishing and picnic cruises were present.

Through training I had learned not to lose my temper when replying to questions from a superior officer so I wouldn't sound insubordinate. It was necessary, I reminded myself, to be careful and learn what was behind this matter.

The general, carrying himself militarily, came in and told me to stand at attention, which I was already doing. He asked for my name, rank, and serial number, which I'm sure he already knew. I felt like a prisoner of war, which essentially I was. He then directed an aide to hand me a V-mail letter.

"Have you seen this letter before?" the general asked.

"I don't recall ever seeing this letter before," I replied truthfully.

"Is this your unit censor stamp?"

"Yes, Sir," I acknowledged, recognizing the imprint with my initials on it.

He asked if I had read and censored the contents of the letter.

"No, sir, I don't read the crew's mail."

"Do you know that failing to censor mail in a war zone is against Army regulations, and is punishable by court-martial?"

"No, Sir," I said, which wasn't exactly truthful, but I had never really been conscious of the law as it might pertain to my small unit.

The general directed me to read the V-mail letter, which was addressed to the Office of Rationing, Sacramento, California, and went something like this:

Dear Sirs:

If my father comes to your office and requests ration stamps to purchase twenty gallons of gasoline for fishing, please give him the stamps because yesterday our air-sea rescue boat used up about 80 gallons, taking officers and their lady friends out fishing.

Sincerely,
Corporal William Chaney, P-399

Shocked, I blurted, "I have never read this letter."

The general's face was flushed, and his eyes protruded from their sockets. I thought he might have a stroke. He screamed at me about letting this letter get back to Air Force headquarters in the states. He kept repeating that he was going to bust me, reduce my rank to private, and send me to Leavenworth. I didn't respond emotionally to his tirade, but calmly answered his questions in a faint voice, even as his anger heightened.

Condemnation of my dereliction of duty—allowing a subordinate to communicate without following proper procedures, my lack of leadership, a failure to enforce discipline, the violation of censorship rules, and conduct not becoming an officer—lasted for about an hour.

Finally the general sent me back to my quarters. The guard took me to the regular mess, not the officer's mess, for lunch. As I entered I was surprised and pleased that the KPs and enlisted men, eating a late lunch, smiled and waved at me. I received several thumbs-up signs. The story had leaked out of the general's office. Didn't they always? At any rate, I had some new friends.

After returning to my hut, I was visited by a major and a captain. I recognized them as having been in the general's office that morning. They used the old buddy-buddy approach to solving the problem. It boiled down to my "voluntarily" assuming all responsibility for the fishing trips, explaining that the short cruises demonstrated how we searched for and rescued downed pilots.

In return, the officers explained, the general would "let me off easy." I would be relieved as skipper of the *Sea Horse* and transferred stateside. I politely thanked them for their intervention and said I would take their proposal under consideration.

Immediately after their departure a tall impressive-looking officer, a full or "chicken" colonel, entered my hut. I think he had been waiting for them to leave. The colonel introduced himself as a liaison officer connected to the Inspector General's Office in Washington, DC, stationed with COMSOPAC (Commander South Pacific) in Hawaii. He explained that Whitey's V-mail letter had been sent from the head of rationing in California to the rationing office in Washington, and, finally, to General Hap Arnold's AAF headquarters. Oh, boy!

The colonel was investigating the situation, heading off any adverse publicity and public relations problems with the media and the heavily rationed American public. I was amazed at how this seemingly small incident had blown out of proportion.

I sensed at once that I had a friend in this colonel and believed that if I were going to escape from this problem, he could make it happen. Recounting the social excursions and our delayed departure for Munda, I explained that the P-399 had been prepared to move for a month. The colonel nodded and said he had some work to do. I assumed he had already met with the general.

After the colonel departed, George and Jep came to see me and said the crew wanted to know why I had been relieved as skipper of the P-399. With a touch of humor, George asked if I was caught selling the *Sea Horse* to the Japanese or smuggling Australian beer without the crew's knowledge. When I told them about Whitey's V-mail letter, George threatened to beat him up—Whitey was only half his size—and to throw him overboard.

I admitted that I agreed with Whitey and wasn't angry about his breach of regulations. Jep said he couldn't believe it had happened, even though he knew I never read the crew's letters home. I simply placed the censor's stamp on them without examination. They were just too personal.

Getting on Whitey wouldn't solve my problem, I said, and asked them to remind the crew how upset they had been after the excursions. They promised not to say anything to Whitey.

Jep related that he had spoken with the skippers and crews of two PTs that had tied up next to the P-399 while gassing up that morning.

They told him about a little-known PT skipper, Lieutenant Jack Kennedy, who had faced a board of inquiry several months earlier after a Japanese destroyer ran over his PT 109.

The board wondered how a slower, less agile vessel could run down a fast, maneuverable PT. An experienced sailor, Kennedy was a courageous skipper who kept his crew together, led them to a small atoll, and awaited rescue. Returning to duty, he commanded a PT 59 out of Rendova before being reassigned stateside.

Jep and George spent over an hour bolstering my resolve to see this through and seek justice before they returned to Lunga in a borrowed jeep.

At about 2100 hours, my guard opened the screen door and in walked the colonel. I was pleased to see him. I thought if he hadn't found facts in my favor he wouldn't have come back.

"This may be my last visit," he said, "so I have to give my instructions to you quickly. Be ready at 0600 hours. I'll pick you up and take you to the airstrip at Koli. I've arranged for you and me to fly to Munda—except I won't go with you. You'll be listed as my aide, rather than by your name.

"When you land," he continued, "go to the Thirteenth Air Force headquarters and see the chief of staff's clerk, a master sergeant. I've wired in code that you will wait for orders transferring the P-399 and your crew out of the Service Command into the 13th Air Force. After the orders are signed, the chief of staff will arrange for you to fly back to Guadalcanal as soon as possible. On a Sunday, you probably won't be missed here. I've dismissed your guard."

Sure enough, I looked out and the guard was gone.

The colonel said nothing about what I should do if caught AWOL, but I could see that this was the only way I could get the P-399 out from under the Air Service Command. I thanked him for his efforts to extract me from a tough situation and said I'd meet him when I returned from Munda—if all went well.

And all did go well. I wasn't asked to sign the passenger list; the colonel had already signed for me. I hurriedly climbed aboard and didn't breathe normally until we were airborne. Two other officers were on the plane and, according to their conversation, were being transferred. The flight was short—a little over two hundred miles—and we put down at Munda airstrip, where I hitched a ride into headquarters with the other two officers.

We had breakfast in the nearly empty mess. I asked a captain dining nearby for directions to the headquarters office. He said he'd take me. After thanking him for showing me the way, I walked into the building.

A corporal drinking coffee offered me a cup. I declined, explaining that I was looking for the headquarters clerk.

"Are you the skipper of the P-399?" he asked, surprising me. "We expected you, but the clerk is over in the mess hall."

So I retraced my steps and found the wrong master sergeant who pointed out the headquarters chief clerk. I went over and stood, waiting for him to finish eating. Seeing me, he invited me to have breakfast, but I declined, explaining I'd just finished.

He had read the colonel's coded instructions and said I could have the transfer order as soon as the chief of staff, a major, signed the document. Snatching the P-399 from under the Service Command amused him.

We walked back to his office and he typed the order of transfer, with two carbon copies. I waited in his office while he went to the major's quarters and had the papers signed, under the order of the commanding officer, a lieutenant general.

The clerk prepared two envelopes, one for the general's office, and one with two copies for me. He called operations at Munda airstrip, and, using his major's name, requested a plane requiring slow time for a flight to Guadalcanal.

The plane was on the apron warming up when we arrived in the major's jeep. I thanked the clerk for his Sunday morning assistance. He responded, "Good luck, I'll see you soon." And off he sped in a cloud of coral dust.

A little later we landed back at Koli airstrip where I bummed a ride to headquarters and returned to my temporary quarters, hoping I wouldn't need them much longer. So far, there was no red alert about my being missing and no guard at the hut's door. I lay down on my bunk and thanked God everything was going as planned. All I could do was wait.

In the early afternoon, a guard appeared and escorted me to the general's office. The same officers were present, including the two who offered me the opportunity to take the blame. A clerk was there to record the hearing. To my surprise and comfort, the colonel from the Inspector General's office was seated near where I stood.

The general entered; I saluted him and stood at attention. He sat behind his desk, appearing less agitated than during my previous hearing. He requested one of the officers who had visited my hut to verify that I had agreed to take full responsibility for the fishing trip, exonerating the Service Command and its staff.

Silence filled the room while they waited. Then I dropped my bomb. I told the major that I hadn't agreed to sign such a false plan and wouldn't retract the V-mail statement.

The general, believing that I had agreed to their plan, exploded, his face turning blue, red, and then chalky white. I don't know whom he was most angry with, his two officers or me. My chicken colonel seemed to be enjoying the scene, and surreptitiously nodded at me.

I handed the orders I had received at Munda that morning to the major, which he opened, reading the order transferring the P-399 to the war zone. I thought he was going to explode. Slowly he handed the paper to the general, explaining that I was no longer under his command.

The general read the order, and his eyes popped out as he glared at me, speechless.

The colonel told the general that, acting for the Inspector General, he had had the orders processed and flown to Guadalcanal. Tactfully, he neglected to say that I had been the carrier. The order restored me as the skipper of the P-399 and directed us to sail to Munda as soon as possible. Finally, the colonel requested transportation for me to return to Kukum Dock.

I refrained from jumping and shouting for joy. I don't think I changed expression, but the general sure did. I was on my way to Lunga Point after

I thanked the colonel again. It was a much happier ride than the one on the way up.

Once back at Kukum, a celebration took place and, even though it was late when I climbed aboard the *Sea Horse*, I fished out the first bottle of Three Feathers to toast our new assignment. The crew wondered where I had procured the whiskey, but I didn't tell them. Whitey apologized for causing trouble, but I encouraged everyone to forget it, adding that they shouldn't write any more poison pen letters unless they told me first.

Later, word reached us that the general had had a P-61 Black Widow night fighter stripped down and converted for use as his private aircraft, allowing him to fly back and forth between Guadalcanal and Australia—until his superiors caught on.

6

Another Storm

THE NEXT MORNING WE FUELED THE *SEA HORSE* AND LOADED WATER and supplies aboard, delaying our departure for Munda. Meanwhile, the weather report was ominous, and the prudent decision would have been to put off leaving.

The crew, however, convinced me to challenge the storm and leave Guadalcanal as soon as possible. They were concerned that the general would reverse the orders for our release and indefinitely detain us if we were still on his island. I was equally anxious to get away from Service Command as quickly as possible.

With reasonable winds and seas, we figured we could anchor at Rendova in ten hours, if we could travel at cruising speeds, but would need help from the weather. Heartened about moving to active duty, although we already had five rescues to our credit, we maneuvered the *Sea Horse* out of the lagoon as we all looked back at the island where victory in the Pacific war had started. Even Danny, our illegal alien, smiled broadly.

With our compass course set, the *Sea Horse* headed toward the Russell Islands, which were about fifty miles away. The Russells were the P-400's new station. From there, we would head for Rendova.

The Japanese used the Russell Islands, located between Guadalcanal and the New Georgia group, to stage troops during the battle for Guadalcanal. Rear Admiral Richmond Kelly Turner, commanding Admiral William Halsey's Amphibious Force, captured the islands in March 1943, a prelude to advancing on the New Georgia group. There was no opposition from the Japanese, who, unbeknownst to the Allies, had left the Russells after departing from Guadalcanal.

Within our first hour, the weather closed in on us and the seas started building. We were in for a long, rough night. Over the next hour we had to cut our speed in half as the seas increased and green water broke over the bow. I knew my decision to attempt the trip had not been sound. We changed watches often, while Jep and I shared helmsman's duties with Danny.

Black skies rolled in from the northeast. The short tropical twilight lasted only moments, and suddenly we were in total darkness. I knew we wouldn't be able to make landfall at the Russells until morning, which meant lying to for the night. We decided to sail toward Rendova off the western shore of New Georgia at low speed. We continued to change watches often, as we battled a headwind. Baker said Salty was sick and wouldn't move from his box bed on the after deck under the awning. Ron and Baker took turns checking on him in between their duties on watch.

No one wanted food, just coffee. We crawled along at about seven knots, still taking water over the bow. The night skies, the storm's thrashing seas, and heavy rains made navigation difficult. I used a seldom-needed directional finder to get an approximate fix on our location and found that we were south of our intended course. I made a cautious correction.

By 0300 hours we noted a break in the storm and seemed to be running out of the worst part of it. Clouds started to scatter and patches of the night sky appeared. The rain stopped and the seas became less rough.

As we were tossed about, riding the bigger waves and crashing through the smaller ones, I was thankful for our experience in storms off Newport Beach in California and Cape Esperance at Guadalcanal. All hands listened for sounds of the surf. It was a precaution we learned from the islanders. Fortunately, we didn't hear any.

It was near dawn when we made out the vague, dark outline of land. Bake and Ronnie had shared lookout duty on the bow all night, lashed to the forward gun mount.

The sky seemed to brighten. Jep kept his binoculars trained on the coastline, comparing the shapes to our chart to identify our location. By good fortune, Hollis received a return radio message from an inter-island supply ship that had a fix on us with its newly installed radar equipment. We were given an approximate course to Rendova harbor.

It was a happy crew, except for Salty, who had not weathered the storm well. We eased through the ships anchored in the harbor and found a small dock where we could tie up to dry out before sailing to Munda. The pier, used by transient inter-island shipping, was temporarily assigned to us by the harbormaster. Otherwise we would have had to anchor offshore.

We radioed operations at Munda and gave them our location and estimated time of arrival the next day. Tired and hungry, we ate and hit the sack.

At noon the following day, we tied up at Munda. I reported for duty at headquarters where I had been the previous Sunday. The crew heard about the V-mail letter and my detention in the mess hall. Staff personnel kidded them about the P-399 being "boat-napped."

I was assigned quarters ashore, but informed air-sea rescue operations that I lived aboard the P-399 full-time and would be standing by for orders. Operations wasted no time, placing us on patrol duty off Kolombangara and Vella Lavella. The Navy provided our supplies.

The Japanese had held the New Georgia group of islands until the previous October when the Allies declared victory after a three-month campaign. US troops landed on New Georgia, the main island, on June 30, 1943, during Operation Cartwheel, a strategy aimed at isolating the Japanese base at Rabaul.

The 13th Air Force was now operating from the airfield on Munda Point, New Georgia, built by the Japanese. This new base was a springboard for carrying out air operations against enemy bases up the island chain.

Our assignment was just what we wanted but we were not seeing much action. Bombers and fighters were making runs over Bougainville, Rabaul, and New Britain, but even though enemy ground fire and Zero-fighter resistance were heavy, we didn't rescue a single pilot or aircrew from the sea. Navy and Air Force PBY Catalinas had picked up downed flyers, but so far we had come up empty after leaving Guadalcanal.

The crew was discouraged because we hadn't beaten other craft to rescue sites. George didn't think the *Sea Horse* was making a top speed of 44 knots in calm water as we had off San Pedro and wanted to get to a small drydock to check the shafts and propellers. Jep and I believed that any loss in speed couldn't be more than three or four knots, but without a measured mile, it was difficult to tell.

7

Special Mission

THE FOLLOWING DAY I RECEIVED NEW ORDERS, A SPECIAL MISSION. FOR the time being there were no additional details; we only knew we were to sail to the Treasury Islands. So we headed northwest from New Georgia to Stirling, the smallest of the Treasurys, which was once part of a barrier reef.

At Stirling we were each given a comprehensive physical examination. All of us were to be immunized for every type of tropical disease, as well as others, and given extensive blood tests for viral and venereal diseases. If the test results were satisfactory, we would receive our orders two days before sailing.

The crew was not overjoyed at facing a week of shots, as they had endured them at Wilmington before shipping out from the states. In California, we all had been ill from these shots. On the other hand, they were glad to have been chosen out of many units to perform this mysterious mission.

Meanwhile Salty became extremely sick. Bake and Ron took him to a nearby station hospital where doctors gave him excellent treatment. But the physicians said stateside dogs were susceptible to disease in the South Pacific's hot climate. Many mascots had perished after a few months in the islands. Dogs bred and raised in the tropics were more likely to survive.

Sadly, Salty didn't make it. The crew buried him while I was at headquarters. Perhaps it was a good thing I wasn't there. It would have been tough for me to hide from them that their skipper had an emotional soft spot for our pet. That evening after dinner I brought out a bottle of Three Feathers and we toasted Salty, whom we would never forget.

Headquarters finally briefed me on our mission, after I convinced the major that the crew wouldn't talk about our mission and that it would make taking shots easier if they knew the reason for them.

The major relented and said our station was Kiriwina Island in the Trobriand Islands—about two hundred miles off the eastern tip of New Guinea—covering the flight paths of fighters and bombers flown from Australia to Munda, or other forward air bases. These aircraft had initially been shipped by sea from California to Australia and prepared for combat. Our station at Kiriwina was about a third of the flying distance from Munda, and a third of the distance from where Australian air-sea rescue coverage ended, south of the Trobriands.

The unusual requirement for shots and blood tests was to protect the islanders, who had no communicable diseases, although they had been subject to some sicknesses, such as appendicitis, malfunctioning organs, and pneumonia. When missionaries in the islands stopped insisting that women cover up their bare breasts with clothing, allowing them to dress as skimpily as they wished, cases of pneumonia were reduced. In that climate, clothing alternated between being wet and dry during the hot and rainy seasons, causing some women to fall ill from wearing damp garments.

The major went on to explain that I would be held responsible for improper behavior toward any woman on the island committed by a crew member. We were not to even look at a female. According to the major, Kiriwinians were Polynesian in appearance, with light brown or olive skin. The women had long black hair and wore only lapas, wraparound skirts made of printed cloth. The men wore short lapas. No one wore foot protection, even on the coral. I informed the crew, and there were a few groans when I got to the "don't even look at a female" part.

It took about ten days to complete the immunizations and examinations. Test results came back twelve days later. All of us were ill from the shots, but we were officially off duty and able to rest until our bodies adjusted.

Summoned to headquarters, the major handed me written orders to proceed at once to Kiriwina Island. Our journey from Stirling Island would cover about 250 nautical miles westward across the Solomon Sea. I was to radio both Australian and Munda operations daily when we went on and off patrol. We were also to monitor our radio each night until all known flights had cleared the area.

I also received the following written instructions:

1. Cooperate fully with the local government, Australian overseers, and New Zealanders stationed in Kiriwina. The island has two kings. Observe and respect local customs for peaceful coexistence.
2. Cooperate fully with the resident missionaries and the operators of their school and orphanage.
3. Do not even look at a female, regardless of any provocative situation.

Special Services provided the P-399 with assorted gifts and treats for the islanders. These gifts were to be used judiciously as trading materials and included candy, powdered milk, small knives, tobacco, trinkets, and items found in ships' stores and the PX store.

We were to save chits and turn them into the finance office, with a copy of our orders, for reimbursement. We learned later that the Trobrianders were the Pacific's most avid traders.

Supplies, including high-octane aviation fuel, would come to us via PBY Catalina flying boats from Australia. The fuel would be dropped in fifty-five-gallon steel drums from low altitudes into the lagoon at Kiriwina. Islanders would float them to our dock with their outrigger canoes. We would use our pump to fill each of our 750-gallon tanks, straining the fuel through a chamois cloth—a long, drawn-out job. It was dangerous on a calm day because of the fumes. When fueling, we flew a red "Baker" pennant, a danger signal, while all hands, except the engineer and oiler, left the boat.

A 110-foot gunboat, the PGM-4, was assigned to escort the P-399 and five other crash boats through the still dangerous seas south of New

Britain and Rabaul, the major Japanese base patrolled by aircraft, including the deadly, heavily armed, four-engine Kawanishi H8K flying boats.

Almost a year earlier, Admiral Isoroku Yamamoto, commander-in-chief of the Japanese Imperial Navy Combined Fleet based on Rabaul, had decided to bolster morale by visiting Japan's advanced bases, including Buin on Bougainville. Our intelligence units had cracked their secret radio code (JN25), which the Japanese believed wasn't possible. This knowledge proved invaluable and was a primary reason we eventually won the war in the Pacific.

By contrast the British cracked Germany's secret radio code by solving the method used by their code machine named "Enigma." The British had a compound at Bletchley Hall, near London, where their decoders used an early one-ton computer called the "Colossus" and a captured copy of the Enigma to solve the Third Reich's radio code.

Alert Allied radio monitors in the South Pacific picked up a secret coded message, giving the exact time that Admiral Yamamoto would land on Bougainville. The 13th Air Force at Henderson Field, Guadalcanal, sent a squadron of P-38s to intercept Yamamoto's aircraft. As the Betty bomber approached the island, our fighters pounced on his plane, killing the admiral. It was a severe blow to the Japanese.

Heavy fighting concentrated on Bougainville and New Britain. American forces levied a heavy toll on the Japanese, cutting their supply lines in northeastern New Guinea near Madang. Things were looking better for the Allies every month.

The skipper of the PMG-4 assigned to sail shotgun for us was Lieutenant (junior grade) Bob Pickering of Burlingame, California. The night before departure I went aboard the gunboat to swap course and speed information with Bob. He told me the weather report warned of a small typhoon bearing down from the northwest, but that it might curve off to the southeast of our course. We set our departure time and planned to rendezvous with the other rescue boats about a mile from our base.

"Why is it that every time we change stations, we have to fight a massive storm to get to where we want to go?" Bake liked to ask.

About an hour out from Stirling Island, winds increased to about fifty miles an hour and the seas began to build. The PMG-4 closed nearer to our course, and it wasn't long before we could scarcely see the other boats in the heavy rain. We reduced our speed to about ten knots. By noon we had only covered about fifty miles and by sundown about another eighty miles.

The *Sea Horse* was riding heavy seas. At dark we radioed Bob that we could no longer see the PMG-4 off our port side and suggested he return to the Treasury Islands. He radioed back that the gunboat would continue on its present course and stay in radio contact.

The storm blew out to the east, but the seas were still running high. At dawn Jep checked our position and corrected our course between two mist-covered islands. Checking our position against Australian charts completed in 1886, we found we had sailed several miles beyond Kiriwina.

We radioed Bob and reported we could not see the PMG-4. I told him we had reached our destination and wished him luck on the return voyage to the Treasurys. We reversed our course and sailed several hundred yards off a reef pounded by the heavy running seas. Finally we discovered an opening in the shoal with calm waters beyond. Steering the *Sea Horse* toward the entrance, we soon sailed wet, tired, and hungry into the most beautiful lagoon we had seen during our South Pacific travels.

We looked at each other and said, "Welcome to Kiriwina."

8

Paradise Found

A VILLAGE WAS NESTLED IN THE COCONUT PALMS FARTHER DOWN THE shore from us. I knew we hadn't made landfall at the main island judging from its size, but rather we had landed in the lagoon of a smaller island group to its south. There was a dock, but I decided to anchor offshore until we received permission to tie up later in the day.

The crew showed the wear and tear of fighting the two-day storm. They looked, and I guess I did too, like a bunch of water-soaked sea otters. We were tired and hungry. Cookie made coffee, figuring we could eat later. All hands changed into dry clothes and hit their bunks, except for Danny, who volunteered to stand watch for two hours.

It seemed I had scarcely put my head down when Danny shook me to report we were receiving visitors. I pulled on a dry uniform, with insignia, and my cap and went up on deck. Jep had asked Ron to make tea. Jep pulled out presents from our ample supply of trading goods.

Arriving on deck I could see an outrigger canoe coming from the village with four passengers and two paddlers aboard. Ron and Bake were topside to help our visitors climb aboard. I looked about and saw that the aft cockpit was shipshape. Danny had obviously worked while his shipmates were getting a well-deserved nap.

An impressive head man, or chief, was the first to climb aboard, followed by two Australian overseers and the chief's assistant. Ron made tea in the last clean pot we had aboard and served it in our sparkling new inspection mugs. Strong black coffee had permanently stained our regular coffee mugs, which had caused us to fail the few, but essential, galley inspections. To correct this, I had traded with Ship's Supply for a set of brand-new cups and stored them below the galley deck for special occasions.

I introduced our crew to the visitors and told them our purpose there was to be on the flight line between Brisbane and the New Georgia islands group in the event planes being flown to Munda went down at sea. One of the overseers explained this to the chief, who nodded in understanding.

I requested permission to use the island dock, with the provision that we anchored in the lagoon when the inter-island supply boat arrived. I also asked for assistance from islanders in securing the fifty-five-gallon gasoline drums that would be dropped by our PBY supply planes and in pumping that gas into the P-399's tanks. I explained to the chief that we would pay in Australian currency or other goods—tobacco, sugar, flour, and small trading items. The chief quickly agreed.

According to his assistant, who spoke English and had attended schools in Melbourne, the chief's name was King Aronging. While the chief understood and spoke some English, his assistant acted as his main interpreter.

After tea, Jep gave each of our visitors a small gift—a small pocket-knife for the king and a comb for his assistant. The king liked the comb so much that we also gave him one. There were pipes and American tobacco for the overseers. As they were leaving, Tom, the overseer who seemed to be head of the Australian advisors, invited me to visit their headquarters for dinner. Once we confirmed the date and time, he said his jeep would pick me up at the dock.

As I watched them paddle over the lagoon's crystal clear, sparkling water back to the village dock, I heaved a sigh of relief and told Jep to send everyone, including Danny, back to their bunks. This time, Bill Chaney took the deck watch. Soon, I was asleep.

Several hours later, we weighed anchor and put the *Sea Horse* along-side the small, sturdy dock near the village. I thought it strange that the villagers had not been crowding their small outrigger canoes around the

P-399. Recognizing that we were exhausted, the king and the Australians likely had suggested they not awaken us.

Mooring at the dock was different. Villagers who wanted to see the Americans covered the entire beach. They didn't attempt to climb aboard, but young and older males and females (*harmi*) jammed the dock four deep. Once again, I reminded the crew not to look at the young girls and women, who weren't the least bit self-conscious about being barely dressed in only a flimsy grass skirt (*rami*), or a sarong-like wrap (*lapa-lapa*). The missionaries on the island preferred the latter. It was not a part of the islanders' lifestyle to be careful of their dress or posture.

The crew probably looked, but there were no incidents. We knew that just one could ruin our entire mission.

We had our first solid food in several days: baked fish with wild lime, taro root, and fried bananas. Most of the village and island population watched us eat. Ron broke out the phonograph and his big band records. He gave our new friends a concert, starting with Bing Crosby and the Andrews Sisters singing "Don't Fence Me In" and the Mills Brothers crooning "Paper Doll." It was a big mistake. The islanders didn't want to go back to the village.

Jep posted the watch schedule. I volunteered for the second dog watch (1800 to 2000 hours). It gave me time to think about our mission and to review and update the boat's log. After Ron turned off the phonograph and the crew went to their quarters, the villagers went home.

Even before we had left the Treasury Islands, Jep, who was generally reserved, seemed quieter than usual. I sensed that something was bothering him, so I decided to talk with him the following day.

The next morning George hit the starter at dawn and the deep rumble of our Hall-Scott engines shattered the quiet, early-morning calm of the village. Many of the islanders came to the beach, as the P-399 headed out through the reef's opening. The tide was high and the *Sea Horse*'s draft was only five feet. We could have sailed across the reef but we only took calculated risks on a "hurry up" mission, so we sailed out the way we came in.

Hollis called operations and cleared our ETA for the flight line. We had a three-hour sail at three-quarters speed to get to the area.

Transfer pilots had the P-399's call letters and position so immediate contact with us was possible. Australian air-sea rescue covered the early part of their flight. The P-399 had duty for the middle portion of their trip, while another AVR 63 covered the final third of the transfer from its base on Vella LaVella.

The South Pacific morning was beautiful. A light sea was running and the *Sea Horse* skimmed the small waves as it got up on plane and we were soon making a comfortable thirty-five knots. If there was a "mayday," pilots knew where we were and could try to fly to our position and bail out or ditch their aircraft.

We had breakfast during the sail out. Afterward Jep and Danny rigged a sea anchor so we could cut our engines and drift slowly. The wind and sea current were light. After the sea anchor was in place, I asked Jep to come up to the bridge.

"What's up?" he asked.

I told him I had noticed something was troubling him. "Are you feeling all right? I realize we haven't received our mail for a month, but squadron operations promised they would check every island post office and when they find it will have it flown to us here."

"Skip, I'm worried about Joyce," he confided. "Not getting mail has made things worse."

I told him Hollis would put a tracer on our mail through command headquarters and try to get an answer. We also decided to have Hollis contact the Red Cross in Hawaii over our liaison short wave set early that afternoon and ask them to check on Joyce. I told Jep I should have spoken to him earlier. In between his official duties, Hollis continued to contact the Red Cross.

On our second day at Kiriwina we were relieved from duty early. All flights had cleared our area so we sailed back to Kiriwina. The break gave us a chance to clean the boat thoroughly, fore and aft; hang bedding off the yardarm; put mattresses on the rail to air out; and scrub the galley, bilges, heads, engine room, and the sickbay.

When we finished I gave the crew shore leave until 1830 hours, except Cookie, who returned early to prepare mess. George and I stayed aboard. Before the crew left for the village, I reminded them to keep their eyes and hands off the village women, that they should be friendly but talk only to men. Some villagers had learned basic Australian English at the missionary school, and a few had attended school in Australia.

As they went up the path to the village I said to George, "Hold your breath." A happy-go-lucky French Canadian, he just replied, "Don't sweat it, Skipper." But I did. Our crew was a high-class group, but they were young and lusty American guys who had been in the Pacific for seven months. I could only hope that looking at these comely, sparsely clothed island girls would not send them off the deep end.

The first good sign was Ron returning with two village youths and baskets filled with our evening meal: cleaned chickens, taro root, and eggs. Ron was all smiles and reported that the fellows were having a wonderful time ashore.

George decided to stroll through the village and said he would walk back with Jep and the rest of the crew. They returned aboard, slightly late, relaxed, laughing, and talking about what they had observed in the village. I was not supposed to be listening, but the "interesting things" they had seen seemed to be size, shape, tilt, and beauty of the breasts on the *harmi*, and the views around the loosely wrapped *rami* and *lapa-lapas*.

The crew had talked to heads of families, who invited them to visit again. They stopped at the missionary's compound and learned about their work with young people on the island. They discovered that *harmi* were frequently mothers at the age of eleven or twelve. Young villagers staying at the compound learned about sports like cricket, Australian football, and spear throwing.

The missionary explained that young people were anxious to return to the village when they turned ten or twelve years old. I told the crew they could regularly visit, signing up by rank for shore leave on a rotational basis. In the meantime, Hollis was still trying to reach the Red Cross for news from Michigan about Joyce.

Our rescue duty was uneventful. Each day we went out to our flight line position. Hollis checked in mornings with our code and an "'Owdy, mite" to pilots as they entered our rescue area. That's the way we liked it, no downed planes.

One evening the Aussie overseers hosted a delectable dinner. There were oysters, Pacific "lobsters," lamb—yes, real lamb, not mutton—and a fruit salad, accompanied by Vickers gin and Foster's beer. After dinner the Aussies smoked American tobacco I had presented to them while we sat back and relaxed in the glow of a beautiful, peaceful island evening. For a brief time, the war didn't exist.

The overseers worked on the island for four-month periods and returned to Australia for four months. The entire group was on the island during the coconut copra harvest season. Their wives did not enjoy island living and remained in Australia for all but three months each year.

They found the islanders to be excellent, dependable workers, and paid a guaranteed amount in Australian currency or living supplies. They worked for Colgate Palmolive Peet Corporation, which leased hundreds of coconut groves on several South Pacific islands. Inter-island ships picked up the copra and coconuts and took it to plants in Australia to process into soap and cosmetics.

In turn I shared our backgrounds and filled them in on our duty to date with the 13th Air Force, including our duty stations. I asked them about the Trobriand Islands, which are located approximately 150 nautical miles from the eastern end of New Guinea and about six degrees south of the equator.

Murua, or as the British named it, Woodlark, was the largest island and farthest east in the group. Kiriwina, located at the northern end of the Trobriand group, was next in size. There were many other islands in the group: Kayleula; Vabuta; and the sacred taboo island, Tuma.

That evening and others during our stay at Kiriwina, the senior overseer told me many fascinating stories about the past and present lifestyles of these quite different people.

In the early 1900s an anthropologist named Bronislaw Malinowski had spent two years on the island attempting to determine where the islanders' original home had been before migrating to Kiriwina. The islanders, he learned, observed a combination of customs from the western Pacific, eastern New Guinea, and the Polynesian islands far to the north.

Margaret Mead had also spent time studying the people and their customs but could not ultimately trace their origins. She worked on only one island studying their traits and traditions, which were not present on all of the Trobriands.

The overseer told me that these islanders were avid traders. In their *masawa* (seagoing outriggers), they set out for distant destinations in the Goodenough and Fergusson islands, which were part of the D'Entrecasteaux chain. On these islands, and Murua (Woodlark), they had trading partners whose locations formed a circle, or *kula*.

Trading began with a gift presentation reciprocated by the receiver. After the exchange, bartering started in earnest, with trinkets, beads, shell necklaces, and earrings changing hands. After each bargaining session, the Kiriwinians would sail to the next stop in the trading circle, which might be as much as a hundred miles distant. The route was either clockwise or counterclockwise, depending on where the *kula* had begun.

The islanders were happy and satisfied people. The overseer said this was because their lifestyle, developed over hundreds of years, had no repression, guilt, or feeling of sin despite missionaries' efforts. Besides, they had the necessities of life, for which they worked, and good health, fearing only broken bones and drowning at sea, a rare occurrence. There was no fear of death.

Their personal and family relationships were interesting to observe. Their government was small, a family-clan type, and was not intrusive but helpful in day-to-day living. Everyone shared in the division of work, from the young to the old. Only in the missionary compound did the young attend school and perform minor jobs.

The women did the gardening, gathered the abundant fruit on the islands, processed sago palm core into flour for various uses, and turned coconuts into milk, meat, and, especially, oil.

Each island hut had several coconut oil lamps burning, and once you experience that scent of the tropics, you never forget it. Washing my hair with coconut oil shampoo, or using coconut-based soap, or eating coconut cake or candy transports me right back in time to the South Pacific islands.

Returning to base after a patrol, we could often smell the island before we could see it if there was an offshore breeze. Coconut palm trees furnished the islanders with a perfect roof covering, in addition to food and light. Overlapping palm fronds over bamboo-like reeds and small limbs, which provided the roof structure of their homes, protected them from tropical rain and storms.

Leased coconut groves all over the South Pacific furnished work for many islanders at harvest time each year. Copra was also a significant product derived from the husk of the coconut.

Island men older than sixteen fished, sailed on trading voyages, or sat in the shade under palm trees and gossiped. Most were tradesmen and performed services for the islanders paid by barter. Some were woodcarvers. Their finished pieces included bowls, fidelity sticks, pain arrows, knives, cooking forks, and betel nut crushers.

Fidelity sticks, carved from eighteen-inch pieces of ebony, were seldom used to persuade a wife to remain faithful. But if a spouse strayed, the betrayed mate was allowed to strike the offender once on the back.

A heavily carved health, or pain, arrow could be purchased, or bargained for, by a villager with a headache. Suffering villagers would take an arrow to the local medicine man who would "remove" the headache by rubbing the villager's head with his hand. The medicine man would then "place" the headache in a pile of sand. Finally, he would spear the pile with the arrow, pinning the patient's pain in the sand. Afterward, the patient would walk away, leaving his headache behind. The overseer explained that, believe it or not, the practice sometimes worked.

The islanders consumed a little alcohol in the form of wine distilled from coconut. Their drug of choice came from betel nuts, which act as a mild stimulant. Some said it was also an aphrodisiac. Kiriwinians smoked or chewed the nuts. Frequent eating of the betel nuts stained their teeth so some islanders chewed the leaf from a vine growing on the island, which offset the staining. I tried it, but spat it out when it burned my mouth and sickened me.

Our Aussie hosts told me about a strong religious belief practiced on the island. Like many religions, they believed in reincarnation, but with one difference. When a person died on Kiriwina, his *baloma* (soul) went to a small island called Tuma, a couple of miles off the northwest corner of their island. It was *gara* (taboo) and considered a holy place, with only priests and other religious leaders permitted to go ashore.

If one of the souls wished to return to Kiriwina, it was made possible by women on the island. A female friend, sister, or mother would shave a spot of hair the size of a silver dollar on her scalp's exact center on the first day of her menstrual cycle. The soul would return and land on the shaven spot. After a while, if the woman conceived naturally and gave birth, the spirit would "return" in the child's form. The mother looked after this baby until it was four or five years old after which time the child would belong to the village.

Everyone fed the child or put it to sleep in their home if it happened to be mealtime or bedtime. Such children were passed from home to home until they were ready to attend the missionary school where they might stay with their mother until freedom beckoned them to jump the fence. Girls left to become mothers and boys to become "night stealers."

"Night stealing" was a dangerous sport in which only the young men of the island participated. A young village boy who could prove he had the most successful stealings was like a football hero on a stateside college campus.

Night stealing began with a young male islander recruiting a friend to be his witness. Next he would select a village maiden and find out where she lived. After dark each evening, he and his witness would lie at the edge of a coconut grove, observing every move the family made, but particularly where each member of the family slept. By custom, men slept on one side of the hut and the women on the opposite side of the open floor sleeping area.

This watch continued each night for a couple of weeks. When the young stealer was sure he knew exactly where his maiden slept, he would wait until the family was asleep, slip into the home, lying next to his prey and letting nature take its course.

Maidens, I was told, seldom cried out or awakened anyone. If a male family member awakened, he would simply roll over and go back to sleep, most likely having been a night stealer once himself. But if a female member of the family—a sister, mother, aunt, or sister-in-law—was awakened, all hell would break loose. The young night stealer would have to run for his life.

The women would chase the stealer, attempting to maim him with clubs they kept just for that purpose. Usually the night stealer would run for his outrigger on the beach to make his getaway. We heard screaming and yelling several times during our stay there. The overseer said the night stealer might not come back to the village for a month, checking first whether it was safe to return.

Night stealing was so prevalent that the headman, or chief, had the island families pick out their most beautiful girl child, based on their standards, about five or six years old, who would become the village virgin. Eight village women guarded this girl twenty-four hours a day until her marriage.

The island tradition of having a young, beautiful virgin of marriageable age had started several hundred years earlier. Over the centuries the Murua and Kiriwina waged war with one another. Marriages between Murua prince warriors and Kiriwina virgins began in the early years when Murua warriors raided Kiriwina, defeating Kiriwina's best warriors. Instead of killing them and carrying off the village women, the Murua demanded a young virgin to take as a bride.

Although victors received their brides, night stealing made it uncertain whether a virgin of marriage age was available when events dictated.

The historic battles, with the sons of Murua kings marrying Kiriwina maidens, were periodically reenacted. Village chiefs sent their sons to Kiriwina for wives to guarantee that no interbreeding occurred.

By agreement the reenacted battles occurred on a Kiriwina beach. A young stalwart would allow himself to be conquered by the invader from Murua, who would demand the traditional spoils of war. Other gifts were also given, including pigs, *massawas* (outrigger canoes), woven bags, carvings, and shell necklaces.

It was a gala occasion, with seagoing *massawas* decorated with vines and flowers around the sail and rigging. There were usually as many as twenty canoes loaded with Muruans, who had bands woven from reeds and decorated with flowers wrapped around their heads, waists, and arms. Islanders prearranged a battle reenactment and the outcome along with details for the wedding and the weeklong celebration.

It was common for us to see an islander weaving a narrow palm frond band or reed around the left arm or the waist of a friend, a significant part of the islanders' dress. Waistbands supported the women's *lapa-lapas* and the men's jock cloths. Both men and women wore a flower like a gardenia in the armband. If they had a mate, their flower looked down, but if they were seeking a mate, their flower was placed in the armband looking up. Men and women also wore flowers in their hair.

As our gathering wound down, the overseer said a wedding was going to occur within two weeks, the second that year. The Australians always assisted with wedding arrangements and the celebration that followed. He said he would arrange to have us attend. I offered our help by providing supplies from our base. I asked for a list of things required for the wedding and celebration.

It had been an enlightening evening and I thanked the Australians for sharing stories about the Kiriwina people. As I left they said they would take me to where the islanders met to dance and listen to native music.

The next day there was still no mail with our supply drop. Hollis tried again to connect with the Red Cross. Jep was disappointed at the lack of news from home. It was early September, and we hadn't had mail since the middle of August. The whole crew was feeling down.

At a meeting in the aft cockpit, the crew asked me to request an assignment in the new combat zones. They thought we were wasting time on this "cream puff" assignment. I agreed and explained that I believed we had been given this assignment as a reward because of the time we had been out in the combat zones.

Earlier, I had requested R and R (rest and relaxation) in Melbourne, about five hundred miles south. There we could put the *Sea Horse* in drydock to make repairs and paint the bottom with copper-based paint. George said he believed we needed to replace the starboard engine and our shafts, which vibrated at high speeds, the result of wear.

Headquarters' reply was simply, "Radio request denied. Proceed to your next mission." Our command must have thought the Trobriands provided enough rest and relaxation.

We had not made a rescue or even been out on a crash mission since leaving Munda. It was a plus that none of the new planes had mechanical defects and flew safely over us and landed in the north. We were much like police or firefighters back home. If needed, we were there to do our work.

Standing by was necessary, but not exciting. I expected reassignment soon. The 13th Air Force had moved its combat units to Los Negros in the Admiralty Islands, linking with the Fifth Air Force and forming the Far East Air Force under the command of General George C. Kenney.

The 13th was a real fighting force under Major General St. Clair Streets, who relieved the great General Hubert R. Harmon. Now we had heavy bombardment squadrons, and tactical control of medium bombers and those terrific twin-tailed P-38 fighters and their pilots.

No crash boats made many pickups off Munda, Vella LaVella, and the Treasury Islands due primarily to the heavy concentrations of various size vessels and PBY aircraft in the Blackett Strait off Rendova and Kalombangara. Submarines also rescued many downed airmen, as did PTs and other larger surface vessels.

The admirals' attitude seemed to be that if a pilot was down, send the whole fleet to pick him up. Air crewmen were our most valuable assets in the push to the Philippines and Japan. Our crew knew that we were part of the 13th Air Force team.

Meanwhile the air war was intensifying. Our P-38 Lightnings and P-51 Mustangs were ripping the Japanese Zero out of the sky. Our flyers had been on wheels when they were three years old, progressing from bicycles, motorcycles, cars, and faster cars to pilot training that prepared them to fly the latest aircraft.

It was thrilling to watch them return to base, sometimes with a double-barrel roll as they passed over the runway, even though it wasn't permitted—and heart-shattering when they didn't return from a mission.

The 13th Air Force—the Far East Air Force—was now, after the New Georgia Islands, on the threshold of the door to victory, but a long, challenging task loomed ahead. It would take all the men, materials, and war supplies available for the Pacific.

The weather in the Trobriands was beautiful for September, with some tropical showers but no severe storms and no weeks when it continuously rained cats and dogs.

There were beautiful sunrises, with colors washing the tropical clouds, and breathtaking sunsets reflecting on our lagoon's glass-smooth surface like spilled cans of gold, red, and violet enamel.

We regularly sat on the deck with conversations conducted in hushed tones or not at all. At sundown I checked the anchor or bow hawser, fenders, the spring lines, the waist, and stern lines, and then did a little paperwork and filled in the day's log. Then we hit the sack.

9

Island Wedding

ONE AFTERNOON WHEN WE TIED UP AT THE DOCK, OUR AUSSIE FRIENDS were there to pick me up for dinner. Our PBY supply plane had dropped the fifty-five-gallon steel drums containing high-octane gas in the lagoon. Jep stayed with the boat to direct the island workers in fueling the *Sea Horse.*

The PBY had also delivered a waterproof "drop bag" with our supplies, but by the look on Jep's face I knew there was no mail. There was just a letter from our operations officer explaining that they were searching the APOs in Rendova and Munda for our mail. They would also try the APO at Los Negros, Admiralty Islands, our new headquarters.

Over dinner the overseer said that when we had finished he would take me over to a *kasayoula* on the other side of the island. A *kasayoula* was a group of different dances for young pre-marriage-age villagers held almost every evening, especially during *melamola* (a full moon). He said instead of telling me about this vital part of island life, they would show me.

During the drive over he said King Aronging had told him that the village virgin's wedding was to be the end of September and hoped we would still be around. I told him I had no idea when we would receive orders to move up but would happily assist with preparations for the celebration and ceremonies.

When we arrived at the *kasayoula lalong* (a grass-thatched hut), he parked about fifty yards away from the dance site. This flat outdoor area was trodden as smooth as poured concrete by hundreds of years of festivals, celebrations, and weekly dances. We walked to the edge of the clearing and sat down along the coconut grove.

We were there only as spectators and were careful not to disturb or interrupt the dances. There was a bright moon low on the horizon. I'm sure the dancers knew we were up there, but it certainly didn't hinder their fun or the dances.

The dance area was about fifty yards from a flat platform made of coconut tree logs, filled and covered with beach sand. It was in the adjacent palm grove and was often used by the island government for meetings and by their religious leaders for ceremonies. The place was called a *dubu* and was considered safe and enjoyed a similar protection to our churches and embassies (even for night stealers, who didn't use its protection often because it was too far from the village). This safe area was part of the dance we later witnessed.

The music was different than what we had heard other evenings on our side of the island. It featured drums of all sizes and tones, and cymbals ranging in size from small to large.

Women flutists were already playing as we sat down by the palms. There must have been a dozen young women playing primitive reed instruments lined up in front of a thatched hut that had drop reed storm curtains. The music coming from these instruments was energetic but pleasant and accompanied by chants sung by the assembled group and the dancers.

The first dance started as six or eight male villagers lined up in a row facing the same number of young *baras* (maiden dancers), scantily dressed and wearing flowers for decorations. The dance, done in time to heavy, compelling drumbeats interwoven with sounds of the high-pitched reed instruments, was very erotic.

The *baras'* graceful motion, starting slowly, was arousing to their partners who gradually moved toward them and then gently pushed away. Their weaving bodies and beautiful, deft flowing hands told their stories, rivaling a French ballet. Spectators were active, singing and applauding the dancers. Young males periodically led a *harmi* (young girl) into the thatched hut to have *mwasama* (fun).

The chanting became more erotic as they progressed. At the height of the emotionally charged dance, the cymbals and drums resounded through the palms, and the *baras* dropped their skirts and stood nude before their partners for a brief moment before bolting up the path to the *dubu*. Of course, the *baras'* partners chased after them.

The overseer explained that if a young girl reached the *dubu* without being caught by her partner, the unlucky young man was not allowed on the platform and was required to return alone to the dance. He also said that *baras* often didn't run fast. We left the singing, dancing, laughter, and *mwasama*, and drove back to our dock.

The next day the Aussies gave me a list of supplies for the wedding and its celebration, including sugar, flour, rice, powdered milk, loose tobacco, no alcohol, and a single flat, white bed sheet.

Hollis raised our supply unit on the radio and turned it over to me to arrange filling this unusual request. I explained what the food drop was for and that it was in addition to our regular supplies. I said our squadron headquarters would understand that this was for public relations purposes and okay the order. In return we would receive two days of free labor from the island workers. That did it, and we received a "roger" over the radio.

At my request, the Aussie overseer made a deal with the king in exchange for their labor.

The next day, after being alerted by radio, our PBY made a special fly-over to drop our mailbag. Talk about an eager bunch of mail hounds (me included, with letters from my wife, Martha, and my parents). Jep was relieved that Joyce was okay, although her letters were dated in August—too early for their child's birth. However, since this was the third week of September, I asked Hollis to contact Radio Brisbane, request that they try to reach the Red Cross in Marquette about Joyce, and radio us with any news.

All of us were happy to receive word from home about our families and friends.

A PBY dropped supplies for the village wedding two days later, which was now six days away. I sent a runner from the dock to tell the overseer that the wedding supplies had arrived, but he knew already. Extraordinarily little happened on that island without him knowing.

The Aussie immediately came over and collected the supplies, which included everything we had requested. The supply unit even sent two white sheets with a note that said, "If you're making up a bed for a VIP, use two sheets, not one. One goes on the bottom, and one goes on the top. They sleep in between." I asked the overseer what the sheet was for, and he said to wait for the ceremony.

Our mission on the flight line remained quiet. And we often returned to base early because the last flights were passing our station at about 1500 hours. Combat-ready facilities, or a sizable portion of them, were moving north from Australia.

The following afternoon the overseer came to the *Sea Horse* and invited us to the village virgin's wedding to the Murua king's son. Kiriwina's king provided a security watch for the *Sea Horse*.

The island's thatch-covered longhouse was the venue for formal weddings. The structure's roof was supported around the eaves by poles spaced about three feet apart. Kiriwina family leaders sat with their backs to their "family" poles. Other male family members sat outside the longhouse behind their leader.

According to the overseer, our crew would have the same status as island families, seated by rank. He also told us about a native drink distilled from coconut milk, lime, and betel nut juice that was a custom at island weddings. "Horrible stuff," he said, "only take a small sip from the cup and spit it on the ground." Refusing the drink was not good public relations. Spitting it out was acceptable.

We thanked the overseer for our invitation to what sounded like a fascinating experience. He asked that we anchor the P-399 at the south end of the beach, clearing the center and dock area for the historical battle reenactment between the two islands as part of the wedding ceremony. The chief didn't think it proper to have an armed foreign vessel at the dock.

Hollis radioed operations about contacting the Red Cross for Jep and learned that the Australian Red Cross was working on it and would call us as soon as they had a message. I requested and received permission for the boat to be on standby Saturday during the wedding, with a crew member monitoring our command radio. We would respond at once to any red flight line alert.

About the same time, operations radioed that they were cutting new orders sending us to New Guinea. Due to a slowdown in Australia's transfer activity, a PBY Catalina unit would cover the upper Coral Sea area after our transfer. The crew was thrilled.

On Saturday, a beautiful tropical sunrise greeted the islanders near the beach, including those who had sailed over from Murua to attend the wedding. The *Sea Horse* crew, except for the radio watch, had a choice spot to observe the mock battle at the north end of the beach. We could see a flotilla of seagoing outrigger canoes nearing the lagoon, with about twenty young "warriors" carrying spears and decorated with flowers lined up on the bows.

The paddlers and their leader—the bridegroom—were in full royal dress and landed the fleet on the beach. The groom leaped ashore and commenced battle with Kiriwina warriors as their ancestors had done centuries earlier. After conquering his foes, he requested a virgin bride from the Kiriwina chief, who announced that the wedding would proceed.

We found our allotted places and felt tension and excitement in the air. As soon as I sat down I spotted the white sheet spread out on the floor in front of the king's flower-decorated chair and realized its purpose. Serving girls, dressed in their ceremonial finery, brought the aforementioned native drink. One of them handed me a half coconut shell filled with the liquid.

I took a small sip, and, with many eyes on me, spit it out on the ground beside me. I passed it to Savard, who swallowed some of it and choked. He passed it along to Jep, who later told me he thought it was like drinking lye. He passed it along, and each man, in turn, spit it out. No one became ill.

Everyone stood as the king, the bridegroom, his father, two brothers, and other leaders came into the *dubu* and took their places.

Music similar to what we heard a week earlier began, while six dancers launched the graceful wedding dance, a perfect beginning to the wedding. When the dance ended, they left with the musicians.

Six islanders from Marua entered the *dubu* and sat in the middle of the floor, facing the chiefs. Following them, a young Kiriwinian, with an excellent physique, came in and stood on our side of the sheet. The overseer said he had heard that the village women knew he was the best night stealer and had selected him for this role in the ceremony.

Only distant sounds penetrated the highly charged atmosphere inside the *dubu*. Then the village virgin bride arrived, wearing a beautiful skirt and flowers around her neck and belt. There were orchids in her armband and her hair. She also wore many *kaloma* (shell necklaces) and *bagi* (bracelets) made of shell disks.

The bride was calm, smiling, and nodded to family and friends. There were no bridesmaids or relatives to give her away. She was a lovely young maiden who had been sheltered against the promiscuous Kiriwinian lifestyle and the night stealers. She had been watched for approximately eight years by eight village women who had not allowed a man or boy near her.

The day after the wedding, these nannies would begin guarding the next village virgin. Murua chiefs had many sons that would come to Kiriwina to "fight" for their brides.

As the wedding commenced, the Kiriwina chief beckoned the bridegroom to his side and directed the bride to lay down on the white sheet, with her head on a garland of flowers. I couldn't believe this was happening. With a motion, he directed the appointed "best man" to kneel before her.

The young man pulled aside her *rami,* with tender non-sensual care. This consummation of two bodies took on a spiritual, non-voluptuous, non-carnal union. There was nothing lascivious about the act. I didn't feel ashamed witnessing this very private union. The Kiriwinians considered it an act of nature.

The bride smiled throughout and only once took a quick, drawn breath. The best man covered her and himself, and then he helped her up, gave her the flowers from his armband, and left the *dubu*.

The chief then brought the bridegroom over to the bride, and they embraced near the sheet that proved she had been a virgin. The groom's father joined them. The two chiefs announced the ceremony's conclusion and invited everyone inside and outside the *dubu* to the celebration.

Music played and there were dancing and singing. As we walked through the village we could see food spread before every hut. The wedding celebration was going to be a long one.

Oddly, the walk down to the beach was quiet, with the crew talking little about the event we had witnessed. We paddled a borrowed outrigger to the *Sea Horse* and brought it back to the dock. The next day we would take on gas and water to prepare for the voyage to our next station.

The crew spent the rest of the evening aboard the boat, talking about the unbelievable things they had witnessed and learned about the beautiful people on this tiny island in the Coral Sea. The wedding celebration lasted all night. The constant sound of drums, gongs, and cymbals could be heard out to sea but didn't interfere with our sleep.

The next morning, as the wedding celebration continued around us, we called operations and received orders for our next station: Los Negros in the Admiralty Islands. Sailing to Finschafen, New Guinea, about 350 miles east-northeast of the Trobriands, we were to pick up necessary supplies and get our bottom painted if a small drydock was available.

After the supply stop at Finschafen, we were temporarily assigned to work with the British at Madang, which was about 160 miles up the New Guinea coast. Upon completing this mission, we were to proceed to the 13th Air Force Headquarters at Los Negros for reassignment. There was a groan when I informed the crew, but everyone accepted the orders without question.

For our last day at Kiriwina, I invited the Aussies to come aboard the *Sea Horse* for dinner. Ronnie had somehow appropriated oysters, Pacific lobsters (no large claws), and fresh vegetables from the local fishermen.

This fare, along with canned meat, powdered potatoes, and powdered milk, made for an elegant dinner.

Dining together for the last time, I thanked our friends from down under for sharing information about the habits, customs, beliefs, and traditions of the people on this small island in the Trobriand group. Except for the overseer, we wouldn't have known much about these happy people.

The occasion warranted breaking out a bottle of Three Feathers, and we toasted Jep's impending fatherhood, hoping that word would come soon about Joyce.

Afterward, we shook hands with the Australians, certain we wouldn't meet again.

10

On to Finschafen

AT DAWN THE NEXT MORNING WE HEADED OUT OF THE SMALL LAGOON with the rising sun's rays glinting along the coral reef. The tropical morning was glorious. Baker came up to the bridge and asked, "Skip, are you sure we're changing stations? Every time we move, we have to do battle with a typhoon." This was a common query whenever we switched stations. I told him not to relax yet because we had a lot of miles to sail and the weather could change.

With a fresh westerly wind and relatively calm seas, I gave Danny the course and the wheel and went below to my quarters to write my report. About the time I got there, Hollis yelled, "Skipper, get Jep! It's coming in!"

I got to the radio fast, and the crew came piling down the companionway. The big liaison set's speaker (our other radio was UHF and was used only for short distance messages by operations) was giving out a steady stream of TWX in code regarding the movement of ships, planes, and troops. Then it came without code.

"St. Bernard [our call name] . . . St. Bernard . . . Do you read us?"

"Roger . . . roger . . . St. Bernard reads your signal and is standing by," Hollis responded.

I looked around at the crew, they were holding their breath.

"St. Bernard . . . Red Cross reports that Mr. and Mrs. George Jepson are the parents of a fine, healthy son, born October 4 . . . mother and baby doing fine . . . end of message . . . over and out."

"This is St. Bernard," Hollis replied. "Thank you, Red Cross, and thank you, Australia . . . over and out."

Then Australia Radio went back to coded war messages.

There were such shouting and laughter, congratulations for Jep, and enough backslapping to put him on sick call. It was October 10, 1944, and the baby was already six days old. You could see the look of utter relief on Jep's face. We all respected his wish to be alone with his thoughts as he went out and sat alone on the bow.

That evening at mess all of us, except Baker, who was at the helm, had a thimbleful of Three Feathers to toast the new father and his brand-new son. Regretfully, it was the last of our secret stash.

Everyone shared in Jep's relief from the worry and anxiety he had been feeling during the last few months. Jep said that he and Joyce had planned, if their child was a boy, to name him George. At the moment, a successful end to this war, a time when we could all return home to pick up the broken pieces of our lives, seemed light-years away.

Finally there was a "Land, ho!" from Ronnie, the forward lookout. We sailed up along the New Guinea shoreline to where we could see, with binoculars, the main harbor with a heavy concentration of anchored cargo ships. I was certainly glad to make Finschafen because we were getting dangerously low on fuel.

We received permission to tie up alongside an inter-island fast supply (FS) ship. We cleaned the boat and our quarters and ate dinner aboard the cargo ship. Sack time came early. We had gotten extraordinarily little rest at sea with the constant checks of the wind, tide, and course.

After the Trobriands we were low on supplies and rations, so the following day Jep and I went ashore to report to the harbormaster and Air Force Operations. To my surprise no one at Finschafen expected us. There was no duty assignment for us. Operations said they would check with Los Negros for confirmation of our orders. I believe we could have sailed to Australia and stayed for a month without being missed. I'll never know.

The supply officer did give us chits for the quartermaster warehouse and supply, and a letter of introduction to ship's stores and the PX. We were given an anchorage assignment, a temporary loan of a vehicle, and told to report back for a duty assignment the next day.

Jep and I headed for the motor pool. Finschafen seemed to primarily be a supply base. There was no visible fighter or bomber airstrip, and it was a madhouse. Roads were congested and dust filled the air so much so that you had to cover your face with a cloth and wear sunglasses for protection.

We both immediately felt the radical change between the peacefulness of Kiriwina and the uncontrolled chaos of traffic between the unloading docks and the storage areas. We agreed that it was good to again feel part of the effort to defeat the Japanese. The crew felt the same way.

The sergeant at the motor pool said he didn't have a jeep, a weapons carrier, or a command car to loan us. He explained that most of these had been stolen, repainted, and hidden by various units. Some were even hoisted aboard Navy ships by cranes, quickly repainted, renumbered, and given to the ship's crew for their use in port.

At Guadalcanal a report showed that more than two hundred stolen jeeps were still on the island. The drivers removed the distributor rotor when they parked their vehicle, and, in the early days of the war, this prevented theft. But then everyone started carrying a spare jeep rotor, so the drivers then had to lug a logging chain and lock with them for the steering wheel to keep the jeeps safe.

With no other alternatives, we climbed aboard a quartermaster-issue six-by-six truck that had seen better days. I started a bucking, coughing engine and immediately realized I had a problem: I didn't know how to drive a six-by-six.

I tried to put it in low gear (the dirty floor mat had a diagram of the gears printed on it). I double-clutched it and got it in gear, creating a near disaster. It was in reverse. I jiggled, pushed, and struggled and finally jammed it in forward gear. A truck rarely runs in high gear at the start (and never on island roads). I kept searching with the gearshift and eventually found low gear.

Finally, with only a little bucking, we rumbled out of the motor pool gate and down the dust-covered road toward the supply unit warehouse. I was embarrassed and felt terrible that I had lost face with Jep, who seemed to think I knew how to do things. I would've liked to hear his version of the "Skipper and the six-by-six," when he told the crew.

Jep, in his usual quiet way, stayed calm and didn't offer back-seat directions. I should have had him drive from the start. However, I learned that before our supply delivery was over, I was much better at backing up the truck than steering it forward.

Collecting supplies took the entire day, but at last we had all the items stowed aboard. Jep and Ronnie looked for a place to park the truck. A Seabee unit let us keep it near their vehicles, and promised to watch it for us, but we still left a threatening note on the front seat.

Early the next morning, we received permission to gas up from a tanker in the harbor, which took half the day.

Operations reported that the P-399 had been temporarily loaned to the British at an installation up the coast at Madang. The type of duty was unknown.

Some of the world's best fighting men—the Aussies and the Anzacs (New Zealanders)—were having a hellish time with a heavy concentration of Japanese trying to cross the Owen-Stanley mountain range, New Guinea's highest, into Port Moresby. The jungle combat was similar to that experienced by American Marine and Army ground troops along the Tenaru, Elu, and Matanikau Rivers on Guadalcanal. These Allied troops were brave people.

Two events delayed our departure from Finschafen.

Staff Sergeant Wilson Hollis, our talented and dependable radio operator and signalman, unexpectedly had to leave the boat and return to the States for medical reasons. Hollis had been with the *Sea Horse* since the beginning. Most important, he was a seasoned veteran and extremely knowledgeable about his role as our radioman. Reserved and quiet, he spent much of his time practicing and studying our codes. He was handy with our signal lamp and flags, and an expert on getting our signal out to our bases and fighter-bomber strip controllers.

Baker had made me aware of Hollis's problem with his kidneys. The entire crew was affected by the day-to-day pounding we were taking in rough seas. There was a constant movement at night to the head or the lee deck. Unfortunately, Hollis's condition was just worse than the rest of us, requiring him to be transferred for treatment.

Before leaving the boat, Hollis showed Jep, Baker, and me the dial settings on our liaison set for San Francisco, Los Negros headquarters, and even Tokyo Rose. Most of us knew how to operate our VHF short wave for various contacts: ship to airstrip base operations, ship to plane, ship to ship, and search area coordinates. Besides his regular duty, Hollis had also taken Danny under his wing, helping him with his English and adjustment to American naval customs. Danny would miss him, and their friendship.

The evening before Hollis left for the States was like a wake. No one could talk about it. I knew these men had a close bond, but this was the first time we confronted it. We suddenly realized that one of us, who had been at our side through trying times, was suddenly leaving our lives. There was little chance we would ever meet again. All we could do was wish him well and talk about getting together after the war was over.

Our new "Sparks" (radioman) would be waiting for us at Los Negros, so Jep, Bake, and I shared the duties of radio operator until then. God help us if we had a heavy-duty.

The second shocker came when I was summoned ashore for a brief meeting with the colonel and a staff member. I thought it was a briefing for our next duty, but I was wrong. Instead, he offered me a promotion to captain, in command of operations and supplies for four air-sea rescue boats. The catch was that I would have to give up my command of the *Sea Horse*, step ashore, and sit behind a desk. A new lieutenant from the stateside personnel pool, or Hawaii, would command the P-399.

Admittedly, I had thoughts about a dry bunk, white sheets, an officer's mess and club, no storm worries, and no need to be on constant alert for reefs, enemy attacks, or operational and mechanical breakdown racing through my head. But it only took a moment to thank the colonel for considering me and decline politely.

Undoubtedly he had a second choice and told me he understood my desire to stay with the *Sea Horse* and didn't press me. Instead, he complimented the P-399, the crew's work, and reputation.

On the way back to the boat, I thought, *Well, there goes my chance to make captain.* Our table of organization (TO) only allowed one commissioned officer per crew no higher than first lieutenant, which had to be the commanding officer. I never regretted making that decision, and never told the crew.

11

Mrs. Roosevelt

THE DAY JEP AND I WENT ASHORE FOR SUPPLIES, THE CREW INVITED some Aussie sailors aboard. These sailors had covered a US Air Transport Command B-24 Liberator bomber flight over the area a year earlier. Mrs. Eleanor Roosevelt, America's First Lady, had been aboard that flight as part of a five-week South Pacific tour visiting sick and wounded Allied soldiers, marines, and sailors in Australian and war zone hospitals.

Several weeks later I met an American seaman who had been at a hospital visited by Mrs. Roosevelt. Everyone had fallen in love with this remarkable woman because she had taken a genuine interest in their injuries and their progress toward recovery. When she returned to Washington and Hyde Park, she had written or called their parents to tell them about her visit with their sons. She was indeed a great lady.

The story circulated that Mrs. Roosevelt wanted to visit the New Guinea coast. Her security people tried to dissuade her, however, because the area near the mouth of the Sepik River was still hot. They told her the only available small boat was an LCM (landing craft mechanized), but there were no facilities aboard. She wouldn't be discouraged and asked them to build a privy on the LCM's stern, with a canvas cover and sides. I never learned if she made that risky trip.

In 1946, a few weeks after my discharge, I was honored to meet Mrs. Roosevelt in Dutchess County, New York, where we resided. I lived in Arlington, a small suburb of Poughkeepsie, six miles from Springwood, the Roosevelt family estate at Hyde Park.

After returning home from the Pacific, our local newspaper printed a news release, written by war correspondents, that overstated my role in a combat action resulting in decorations for our crew. A longtime friend and politician insisted I run for a county commission seat as a Democrat, an offer I refused. After three years in the service, I had only been home about a month and was just starting civilian life. I didn't want to become involved in politics.

Unfortunately, local newspapers carried stories that I was a candidate for county office. I didn't want to give my political friend a tough time, so I called him and said I wouldn't participate in the campaign.

One day, he phoned and asked me to join Mrs. Roosevelt on a program aired on WKIP, our local radio station. There was no way I could refuse the offer. Despite my inexperience as a speaker, the program went quite well.

Later in the year the president of the Dutchess County Women's Democratic Committee invited me to speak at a luncheon. I hesitated until she told me that Mrs. Roosevelt would be there. On the day of the luncheon, I met beforehand with friends over coffee. I was wearing a brand new, tailor-made suit (the first and last, I ever owned).

When the time came for me to leave for the luncheon I stopped in the men's room. As I was about to come out, I discovered that the fly on my new trousers wouldn't zip. I tried and tried to no avail. I went to my car parked near the restaurant and got a pair of pliers. Again I tugged and tugged with no luck. I could only guess what people thought as they passed by. Time ran out and the zipper still wasn't fixed. I walked into the luncheon with my hands strategically placed in front of me just in case my shorts began to show.

Sure enough, Mrs. Roosevelt and her daughter-in-law, movie actress Faye Emerson, were seated two chairs from me. When I was introduced, I stood and held a large napkin in front of me, unobtrusively, and made a concise speech.

In her very gracious way, Mrs. Roosevelt said, "It's good to see younger candidates do not get carried away with long speeches." If she had known about the zipper, I believe she would have laughed.

12

The British

OUR BRIEF ASSIGNMENT FOR THE BRITISH WAS REMARKABLY UNSUC-cessful. We tied up at their small dock near the commandant's headquarters in Madang, and I reported. A young corporal, who led me to the major's office, kept calling me "leftenant," a title I was not familiar with, but I overlooked it.

The major was sitting at his desk and left me standing at attention while he, with his head down, read something on his desk. I felt this behavior was rude. After much throat clearing and "gahumphing," from me, the general looked at me and gave me an "at ease."

Our mission for the British was reconnaissance—sail up the Sepik River, near Buna, west of Madang about ninety miles, on New Guinea's north shore.

The Japanese had a major concentration of troops in the Sepik River basin. The Australians and New Zealanders had performed a remarkable job of keeping them confined to that area, preventing them from crossing the mountains to the island's south shore and Port Moresby earlier in the year.

General Douglas MacArthur had bypassed this enemy force and several Japanese-occupied islands to the east and north. Some, including troops at the Sepik River, had set up a military perimeter around a useless portion of the island, minimizing their ability to receive supplies. As a result, they were no longer a fighting force, merely a threat.

Allied airpower had grown more robust, forcing the Japanese to convert valuable warships to supply vessels in an attempt to get food and ammunition to these troops. The British and Australians wanted information about bombed-out docks up the river. Photos taken from the air could have provided that knowledge, so I was a little skeptical about the mission.

After receiving verbal orders, I left the command office and went back to the P-399, trying to sort out the details and mixed thoughts about the mission. The facts didn't add up. Why did the British request a US crash boat? There were two British boats anchored near us. They were used to take supplies, mail, and passengers between islands, but could have easily performed this job. Was it because we were faster and more heavily armed? Why had the major emphasized that he wanted a report regarding the inland Sepik River shoreline? How far up the river?

When I was back aboard the *Sea Horse*, Jep and I discussed the mission. "This doesn't look good," he said. "There could be a catch, so let's be cautious."

The rest of the day we took on water and gassed up (their fuel, which was, at least, free). The armament was clean since we hadn't had daily machine gun practice or general quarters drills since we left Kiriwina. We were ready for an early departure into who knew what.

The voyage west to the Sepik River mouth was uneventful. We sailed as close to shore as possible. The dense jungle growth stretched from the shoreline to forbidding mountain peaks rising out of the middle of this vast island, which was 70 percent wilderness forest.

New Guinea was the beginning of Melanesia (Black Islands), where dark-skinned east Asians had inhabited its shores for more than 25,000 years. Melanesia includes many islands that stretch east to the Solomons and Fijis. Descendants of these people were sprinkled throughout most of Micronesia (islands to the north and northeast) and in a few Polynesian groups in the northeast Pacific, including the Hawaiian, Gilbert, and Marshall groups. Some settled in these widely spaced islands as far back in history as 3000 to 2000 BC.

The island stretches from the Coral Sea westward about 1,400 miles, is narrow (averaging about ninety miles wide) on its extreme east and west ends, and is up to 280 miles wide in the center.

The government was split, with Australia governing the eastern half (Papua) and the Netherlands East Indies governing the western half (Irian Jaya). Its western tip was only fifty miles south of the equator, and its eastern end about 650 miles below the line.

New Guinea covers 270,000 square miles, and its people are the least understood of our last frontiers. The lack of worldwide interest in its 40,000-year-old culture largely isolated the island. It had a hazardous and challenging environment to explore and an ecosystem that didn't easily lend itself to more dense population growth. Living conditions didn't encourage exploration or searches for minerals, oil, and other natural riches.

Few explorers had penetrated this strange otherworld and returned with the story of its primitive existence, which was very much the same as it was a thousand years ago.

New Guinea also presented health concerns. Like most islands, malaria was prevalent. The *Sea Horse* crew had had it and knew what a toll it took on one's stamina and energy. The fever and chills hit you at time intervals, sometimes every four, six, eight, or twelve hours, and could flatten you.

There were well-worn trails up and down all sides of these mountains. Living customs varied widely between villages and small family communities, which varied with the culture and lifestyles of the villages down on the flatland and seashore.

New Guinea teemed with wildlife because there were few natural enemies or carnivores. Wildlife on the island consisted mainly of cassowaries; tree kangaroos (lousy climbers); crowned pigeons; other species of birds and parrots; birds of paradise; and, of course, snakes. Flowers were in abundance, with hundreds of beautiful species, including an uncountable number of orchids. Leaves and bark from many trees and plants were used for medicinal purposes.

There were dozens of tribes on New Guinea. As we later journeyed westward, and farther along the island, we learned more about these Melanesian people by speaking with Australian and Dutch government representatives and reading reports on the life of a few of the tribes in the lowlands and the mountains.

There was a noticeable difference between the self-government, the social structure, family unions, and male-female status from village to village and tribe to tribe. The lowland people had customs different from those of the mountain people.

In some villages, the men lived in community housing and the women, including wives, ate and slept together. The men hunted birds and wild boar and fished. The women gardened, made sago flour, and gathered fruit. The women in some tribes grew taro root, sweet potatoes, and cucumbers. And they gathered nuts. Women also tended their most valuable possessions, pigs, which were highly prized dowries for brides.

Jep and Baker had their binoculars trained on the shoreline, scrutinizing every village and passing native fishing vessel, and, of course, the open sea ahead.

As we neared the mouth of the Sepik River, brown water fanned out for a mile or more into the sparkling blue-green of the sea. Jep came to the bridge and said we'd better make a wide swing around the brown water. Short coconut logs about three or four feet in length were everywhere.

It finally struck me why the major wanted "Leftenant" McCandlish to sail the P-399 up the Sepik River. He didn't want to risk one of his boats. The Japanese were chopping down coconut palm trees, using forced local labor, and tossing them into the water to block Allied boats from coming up the river. The logs would ruin propellers, shafts, and rudders.

Shifting the *Sea Horse* into neutral, we drifted while I looked up the river and along its banks. Logs floated all over and under the muddy water. Some had drifted a couple of miles out to sea.

Any boat entering this area would have little chance of escaping undamaged. Bends in the river were also a natural spot for a Japanese ambush. The logs' presence caused me to conclude that the Japanese were not expecting to receive supplies or reinforcements via the river route. They had cleverly closed it to small war vessels, such as PTs, gunboats, and air-sea rescue boats like the P-399.

Using our two pike poles, we pushed the short logs away from our hull as we edged our way back down the coast until we knew we were free of the Japanese "confetti."

Returning to Medang late, we anchored away from the headquarters dock. I didn't do this as a deception but couldn't help it if the British major's staff thought we were returning from the Sepik River when we tied up at their dock about noon the next day. I reported and saluted the major, wondering whether his face had flashed a brief look of surprise. His expression was usually unreadable.

"Well, leftenant, what do you have to report?"

I told him about the floating barricade of logs and other debris at the mouth of the river, explaining that, in my judgment, attempting to navigate through the obstacles would have risked severe damage to the *Sea Horse*'s propulsion. I added that we observed no signs of wharves near the river's entrance.

There was a long pause in the conversation, a clear sign that he was not pleased that, despite the logs, we hadn't gone up the river.

He said the reason we were assigned to this mission was that we were small at sixty-three feet and could go around the floating chunks of wood. *Aha, he did know about the logs and hadn't told us beforehand.* The major said he would have to forward an unfavorable report to my commanding officer.

Without saying a word, I saluted and left.

13

Los Negros

We gassed up, put food rations aboard—at least we got that from the British in return for our time and effort—and reported in code via radio to our headquarters in Los Negros.

The radio message was our first since Hollis had left us, and it worked. I regretted that the unfavorable report about us from the British would show on our record, but I still felt we had used proper judgment. I had also requested that our new radioman be ready to join us when we reached Los Negros, and said we would stand by for further orders.

In Finschafen I learned there were at least two other air-sea rescue boats stationed at Los Negros, so I knew we wouldn't be needed there.

The next morning, we set our course for Manus, Los Negros, in the Admiralty Islands. The voyage was only 160 miles and we could make it in about six and a half hours with fair winds and a choppy sea running. Jep talked with some British seamen who warned him about the treacherous reef surrounding the island's anchorage.

PT boats continually tried to sail over it, according to the British, ripping out their bottoms, rudders, shafts, and propellers—even at high tide. At low tide, any vessel in the same area would be sitting high and dry on black lava rock.

I found the information helpful because the charts issued for that area were old. Over time, coral could grow several feet on top of the volcanic base. There were other similarly unreliable depth readings throughout the South Pacific.

We made landfall about two miles off Manus, Los Negros, and could see many large cargo ships, which appeared to be anchored together in deep water. But our vision was deceiving. The Liberty ships unloading were actually near shore, inside the treacherous reef. Other vessels waiting to unload were on the seaside of the reef.

To enter, we had to sail to the extreme south end of the harbor and ease through a small opening in the reef. The chart did not show channel buoys, or danger buoys, to help navigators. We made it safely into the harbor and sailed down to where the other air-sea rescue boats were tied.

A sailors' reunion ensued when we joined them. Most of the crews had gone through the Higgins' School together in New Orleans, and this was the group's first reunion since.

At headquarters I reported to the colonel, filling him in on missions at Kiriwina and with the British at Madang. His only comment on our negative report from the British major was that we had used good judgment not to take the *Sea Horse* up the Sepik River "under the described conditions." Then he handed me a personnel file and sent for Hollis's replacement.

Reuben Barzow, a young man from the Bronx in New York, immediately impressed me with his directness and apparent ability to handle the communications job. Time would tell if he could meet Hollis's exceptional performance in storms, combat conditions, and under pressure in general.

Knowing VHF, HF, IFF, secure codes, signal lamps, and grid coordinates and maintaining liaison with air traffic and base tower controllers were no easy tasks. And if this wasn't enough, the radioman's duties in an emergency might include turret gunner, aiding the mate in taking bearings at the helm on long inter-island voyages, bow watches, and assisting in anchoring where necessary during search and rescue operations. Simply, each member of the crew had multiple duties.

While operations cut our orders, Barzow and I walked down the beach and sat on a fallen sago palm tree to get further acquainted. Like most of us, he landed in air-sea rescue boats by pure chance. After enlisting, he was assigned to the Signal Corps, where he studied Navy signalman duties and learned about radar, the recent technology. Crash boats were considered too small for this invention that many claimed won the war.

Barzow's records showed he had a high rating in his MOS (military occupational specialty). I believed he would fit in with our crew. We lived together like a family on a sixty-three-foot boat, sleeping, eating, and working.

The rare occasions when we had leisure time, we played cribbage and gin rummy and sailed our eight-foot dinghy. Sailing along reefs gave each crewman a chance to be alone with his thoughts and observe the magnificent underwater life. Later we beached the dinghy when it interfered with our eight-man inflatable raft and its five-horse Evinrude outboard motor.

Our wind-up phonograph and a wide selection of big band 78 rpm recordings helped make the days a little more pleasant. To this day I can't hear the first three bars of a Goodman, Dorsey, Ellington, or Miller recording without being transported back to the afterdeck of the *Sea Horse*. These songs, along with those by Bing Crosby, the Andrews Sisters, and the Mills Brothers, eased our daily life in the South Pacific. Duke Ellington's "Take the A Train" was a particular favorite.

After Jep met Reuben, he told me we were fortunate to get him. When he came aboard, Jep gathered the crew to welcome him. It wasn't long before our new "Sparks" became an integral part of the *Sea Horse* family.

Our orders were to return to New Guinea's north shore, with stops at Wewack, Aitape, and, finally, Hollandia, the staging area for General MacArthur's invasion of the Philippines. Once there we would receive orders for our next mission. Our war was about to heat up. We refueled and took on provisions and supplies for the sail back to New Guinea.

Early the next morning, as the sun broke on the horizon, flooding Los Negros, Manus, and the other Admiralty Islands with brilliant tropical rays, I set a course for Wewack. Our landfall was just west of the Sepik River's mouth, the same area the British had sent us. After a short stay there, we sailed westward to Aitape, a distance of about 130 miles.

At Aitape we reported on the vessels we had observed in the small ports along the shore. Our next destination was Hollandia in the western half of New Guinea, under the Netherlands government. Hollandia Harbor was rapidly filling with invasion forces staging for the pending assault on the Japanese-occupied Philippines.

During our passage we found a small island with a freshwater stream gushing out of the hills. Baker tested its purity, and when we determined that it was safe, we drained and refilled our water tanks. All hands enjoyed a rare freshwater shower. The only other times we had freshwater showers were during line storms.

We also washed the *Sea Horse* fore and aft, aired our bedding over the cable rails, cleaned the bilge, polished the brass, and coiled the lines. It was dark before we sat down to a mutton dinner.

The next day Jep, Baker, and I visited two villages. The inhabitants were Papuans, whose basic living had remained about the same for hundreds of years, with the only changes brought in by outsiders, such as metal tools, manufactured bowstrings, and matches.

The British and Dutch had outlawed village raiding, including the rape and stealing of women, and, of course, the ritual eating of "long pig" or cannibalism. Cannibalism carried a punishment of death by hanging. As late as 1969, two missionaries were kidnapped, roasted, and eaten by central mountain islanders. On the north shore in 1998, twelve young islanders were reportedly killed and eaten.

The indigenous people painted their bodies with a crushed white coral lime paste and berries. Face and body jewelry made from bones was popular among the Papuans. They ate a bountiful diet, mainly of yams and other garden-grown vegetables, such as taro root and cucumber. The women also made sago palm flour bread. Coconuts had many varied uses, including as sustenance. Additionally, their supply of fresh fish from the ocean and streams, an occasional pig, and edible birds made the food supply plentiful.

We decided to report to Hollandia early and find a unit that might help us secure a replacement for our starboard engine. George had been warning me the starboard engine might break down, as both of the Hall-Scotts were well beyond their running time between overhauls and required replacement parts. The Navy at Hollandia might be able to help us. We could use the extra time to procure supplies and prepare the boat for what might be another long stretch of hard sailing farther up in the war zone.

We were still at Aitape when trouble hit us like a five-inch shell. At about 2100 hours, Baker came to my quarters and reported that Danny had sharp pains in his lower right side and was running a fever. He said Danny hadn't been feeling well but hadn't told anyone. Baker said he was sure it was appendicitis and we had to get him to a surgical unit as soon as possible.

Barzow radioed area installations to locate a station hospital and arrange to get Danny to a dock where an ambulance could meet us. I told him to use our secure codes but if he wasn't getting through to put our request on open VHF channels to all ships and installations—to use all means short of sending out a "mayday"—and even that later if necessary.

I went to the crew quarters to see Danny. He was in a lot of pain even though Baker had given him a sedative. We moved him to sickbay, where he would be more comfortable while Baker looked after him. I told Danny that we were working on getting him to a doctor.

I joined Barzow who was checking with Wewack and Aitape installations, but so far, he hadn't come up with local help. Then he called the port officer at Hollandia. After several repeated requests for medical assistance from shore units, we thankfully received a response from a standby radio operator on the US hospital ship *Comfort*. He requested our coded position, speed (over the bottom), and range (we checked our gas tanks, which were in decent shape). He asked us to standby.

The whole crew was concerned for Danny and encouraging him. We held our breath, waiting to hear whether the *Comfort* was within our range. After a few minutes, their radioman gave us their coded position and passed the word from their navigator that if we were ready to sail, our estimated arrival time would be about one and a half hours. The *Comfort* was lying off Hollandia, where it could be available to the invasion fleet.

George had already warmed up the engines. Only a light sea was running, so we could take advantage of our speed. That was the longest hour and forty minutes I could remember. Finally, Jep spotted the ship's running lights with his binoculars. The beautiful white ship with the prominent Red Cross symbol painted on its hull was a welcome sight. Hospital ships could be lit in war zones. Under Geneva Conference rules, the Red Cross symbol was supposedly off limits. On December 12, 1944, a couple of months after we put Danny aboard the *Comfort,* the Japanese reportedly fired on this vessel, or her sister ship, *Hope.*

We broke out a wire litter, gently placed Danny on it, and carried him on deck. I got a hail from the *Comfort*'s lower deck and brought the *Sea Horse* around to a boarding hatch on the lee side near the stern of this massive ship. The officer of the watch expected us and lowered snatch blocks with tackle down to our deck, which was riding nice and level.

Jep didn't hook the blocks to the litter right away, giving each of us a brief moment to say a final goodbye to our shipmate and friend. Danny was a highly decorated citizen of the Netherlands, and, of all things, due to be arrested by US Immigration as an illegal alien, if ever they could catch him. I placed his personnel file in the litter and they hoisted him aboard the hospital ship. Jep sent up his seabag on one of the tackle hooks.

We never saw Danny again, but we all felt good that we had gotten him the best medical care in the war zone. Barzow tried several times over VHF to inquire about Danny aboard the *Comfort* but wasn't successful.

Before Danny's illness, I had planned to contact a Dutch government office in one of our ports in the Netherlands East Indies. West New Guinea, Borneo, Celebes, and the Molucca Islands were all Dutch-mandated territories. I believe they would have assisted Danny with our immigration department, or perhaps put him under their diplomatic care. I never had a chance to speak with him about it.

The crew stood by the rail as I eased the P-399 away from the *Comfort*, set a course for Hollandia, and sadly looked back at that beautiful ship.

Pacific war histories contain so little about these great mercy ships that saved thousands of civilian and military lives. In 1944 there were three new hospital ships—*Hope*, *Comfort*, and *Mercy*. All three were built in Wilmington, California, by Consolidated Steel, practically next door to Fellows & Stewart who built the *Sea Horse*. There was also an older hospital ship called the *Solace*, which had been a converted Navy vessel.

The mood aboard the *Sea Horse* was somber after we left Danny aboard the *Comfort*. It's difficult to explain the deep and long-lasting feelings for our shipmates Danny and Hollis. Bonding in friendship is unique among men in all armed services units, where your life is in the hands of your mates.

14

Hollandia

Sailing into Hollandia Bay the next day, we found the harbor teeming with what seemed like a thousand ships, waiting for the thrust north to liberate the Philippines and destroy Japanese bases in the Western Pacific. This scene shook us out of the gloom caused by losing Danny.

The high shoreline on both sides of the harbor entrance concealed the tremendous buildup of ships of all classes and sizes, loaded with troops, mechanized equipment, guns, ammunition, and support supplies. The anchorage extended as far as we could see to the village of Hollandia.

We had learned in Finschafen that all roads (or shipping lanes) led to the Western Pacific and the Philippines. General MacArthur's plan was underway to bypass large numbers of Japanese troops on islands and areas on the north shore of New Guinea, where they could not be supplied and supported by Tokyo. This strategy eliminated vast numbers of Japanese as a force.

The 13th Air Force, the 5th Air Force, and equally courageous Australian and New Zealand pilots drove the weakened Japanese land-based aircraft squadrons to their northern bases.

Allied forces were spreading to the western end of New Guinea, Biak, Sansapor, Noemfoor, and Middleburg Island. Air supremacy made it possible for our forces to attack and destroy oil wells in Borneo, a large part of the fuel supply for the Japanese war machine. Taking western New Guinea also gave us bases from which to invade Morotai, a critical crossroads on the path to the Philippines at Mindanao.

The Rising Sun was beginning to feel the crunch and slowly crumbling.

Once assigned an anchorage, Jep and I inventoried the boat's needs to determine what to requisition to replace or repair worn and defective working parts. Along with George, we spent most of our time on the beach, acquiring items at supply terminals.

Our shopping list included one intercom radio for Barzow, one five-cubic-foot refrigerator for Ron, assorted medical supplies for Baker, .50-caliber ammo for our twin turret guns, 20-mm ammo for our seldom-used small cannon, small arms ammo, maintenance supplies, one Onan five-kilowatt generator, twelve-volt batteries, Navy blankets, and four new 78 rpm big band records.

George requisitioned a new Hall-Scott engine, two new shafts, two struts, one new solenoid (gearshift), and one spare propeller. Supply denied our request for small radar equipment and a smokescreen mortar.

I had little hope we would get the much-needed engine and parts, and expected supply to say, "Get a new boat." But George and Bill Chaney found a civilian factory engineer from Hall-Scott. To my surprise he arranged for the replacement engine, shafts, struts, and a prop to ship from the US to our next station, where a crane to lift and lower it was available. Only good luck and perfect timing would make this repair work successful.

Our next station was Biak, where bombing flights to the Halmahera and Celebes islands began. With this knowledge, we arranged with the Navy to transfer a small drydock there, paint the *Sea Horse*, and replace the engine and shafts. Having the opportunity to refresh the boat and replace the engine was a huge relief.

At night, the constant churning of ship-to-shore tenders nearly ceased, and a calm descended over the harbor. Only blinking signal lamps broke the evening darkness, like so many fireflies. Bright lights illuminated the shore and silhouetted the hulls of the anchored ships. The lights on a hill twinkled from General MacArthur's new home and headquarters.

MacArthur had recruited Seabees and other hard-to-get craftsmen (carpenters, electricians, plumbers, and masons) to build his home at Hollandia. GIs living and sleeping in basic surroundings resented his flamboyant war-zone lifestyle. Rank had its privileges.

With all of our tasks finished at Hollandia, we weighed anchor early in the morning and headed west, in clear weather, along the stunning New Guinea shore. Seas were relatively calm and winds were light.

I set a course and, with Jep on the bridge, we made excellent time over the bottom. In the afternoon I was working on a report. We had been sailing about seven hours when Jep came to me and said, "Skipper, I think we should check our course for Biak."

A bearing on a small island off our starboard bow showed we were far north of our correct course. We went down to the charts and then took binoculars up to the bridge. Sure enough there was an island quite some distance south of my calculated course. So, the big island off our port bow must be Biak. I had calculated that Biak would be well to the northwest of our present position.

How easily your navigation calculation can become questionable. I prided myself in reading the sailing conditions, speed, and setting compass courses. I believed my course for Biak was correct. I just couldn't understand it, but there was that small volcanic island, which showed we were too far north, so I reset our course for the southwest and what had to be Biak.

We made landfall at the eastern end of this mysterious island and cruised up its south shore at idling speed. Strangely, I didn't see signs of a military installation or flags fluttering above the palm trees. Finally I spotted, as did Jep and Barzow, a barge, some huts on the shore, and a group of Japanese soldiers strolling down to the beach to see the boat approaching their dock.

General quarters! This was a Jap island!

I threw the throttle to full ahead and crash-turned the P-399. In a minute we were approaching forty knots, with no shore guns firing on us. Apparently the Japanese were as surprised as we were. The island turned out to be Yapen, inhabited with several thousand bypassed Japanese troops. Was I glad to escape from that navigational error.

So, what had gone wrong? I put the *Sea Horse* on a course that intercepted our original, and, after double-checking the charts, the answer came to me. There was a second island, not shown on our chart. Aussie charts drawn in the late 1890s didn't show this island because it hadn't yet formed.

With its many volcanoes, the South Pacific spewed out lava to make new islands and enlarge older ones. Coral would grow and trap sand, then coconuts from other islands would float from miles away, land on this new shore, and start a palm grove. Newer charts included some of these more recently formed islands.

Not long after our detour we sailed into the anchorage at Biak, which was bristling with activity, and this time we saw the US Navy—not Japanese soldiers.

The next day Jep and I borrowed a jeep at the motor pool to tour the installation on the island and check whether anyone knew where our stateside supplies would be delivered. Supply told us to come back in about three days, which would give stateside time to notify them about the delivery schedule, whether by surface or air. We also arranged for gas and food stores.

The *Sea Horse* and our crew appeared to be Navy (the crew generally dressed as working seamen in dungarees and dixie cup hats), so everyone in our docking area believed we were Navy personnel and invited me to the Navy officers' mess and club. The crew went to the Navy seamen's mess for a good dinner.

One evening I "promoted" Jep and Baker with my old second lieutenant's bars and we all went to the officers' mess together. We had an enjoyable time but when we got back to the *Sea Horse*, Jep and Bake said they would be more comfortable going to the enlisted seamen's mess and club. Barzow, Ron, and Chaney said the enlisted mess's cooks were better than the officers' mess.

Jep would have made a great skipper and had turned down a promotion to warrant officer in his first few weeks aboard the *Sea Horse* back in California. But he was in the service to do a job and liked his role aboard the P-399.

We arranged to have a small drydock used primarily for PT and landing craft repair towed up to Biak from Hollandia. We also found an anchorage near an unloading barge crane that could lift the boat into the drydock.

Once the *Sea Horse* was in the drydock, all hands turned to scraping and caulking the double-planked hull and painting the bottom, below the waterline, with copper-based paint. Copper paint prevented sea worms from eating the wood, just as termites eat building foundations onshore. Then we painted the *Sea Horse*'s hull, decks, and superstructure with dark gray marine paint.

George received a call from the supply notifying us that the new engine and shafts had arrived by air from Hawaii. Replacing the worn-out engine took time because we had to open the deck, built to accommodate engine changes by a smart boat builder.

We completed the change without problems. It was about 120 degrees in the engine room during the day. George was an excellent small engine mechanic who spent twelve years in the Navy at Pearl Harbor before the war. He loved to tune, adjust, and continuously test the operation of his "babies."

He was unhappy because we couldn't attain the *Sea Horse*'s top speed of forty-four knots (initially set along Point Fermin's measured mile near San Pedro) after arriving in the South Pacific.

We checked the boat's speed off Taivu Point, Guadalcanal, in a measured mile set up by the Corps of Engineers. Over time there had been a corresponding lowering of our speed at all engine rpms. This lack of actual speed knowledge, taking sea, wind, and current conditions into account, affected our dead reckoning and our ability to make an exact landfall.

It was a red-letter day when we put the deck section back in place, sealed and painted. Every man had put out 150 percent to get this weighty job done. It was time for a celebration, as we put the *Sea Horse* back into the water. It looked beautiful.

By luck a USO show was playing at the Navy base. The shore patrol put a guard on the P-399 and a new friend at Navy operations provided chits (permits) for the crew, so we all could attend. It was an excellent reward for the crew.

This USO show had been giving performances all over the South Pacific, and, like many of the shows that toured the war zone, had no blockbuster stars like Bob Hope, Jack Benny, or Betty Grable, but the guys on the island couldn't have cared less. They were a terrific audience.

The show featured two comedians, talented musicians, female dancers, and starred Viki Weems, from Dickson, Tennessee, who danced a great hula and sang the always popular "Embraceable You." She left the Seabees and engineers howling for more.

Afterward a Navy friend mentioned that Jack Benny had given a great show at one of their previous bases, with movie star Carol Bruce as its main female attraction. She came on stage dressed in a skin-tight dress, which beautifully displayed every delicious curve. She wiggled as she started to sing, "Birds Do It" and the place went wild, my friend said, but was nothing compared to the howls that erupted when a New Guinea beetle, the size of a silver dollar, flew into the lights and landed on her pubic area.

She was petrified, screamed, and tried to knock it off. She was afraid to touch it and tried to burlesque bump it off without success. Jack Benny came on stage to help, but she wouldn't stand still. Then to complicate the situation, a burly Seabee jumped on stage, in front of Benny, and tried to pick the bug from her. She was more afraid of the Seabee than the bug.

The drama came to a howling conclusion when Patty Thomas, a dancer with the show, saved the day by grabbing Bruce's waist to hold her still long enough to gently remove the beetle from her fellow performer, who left the stage and didn't return. Benny thanked the Seabee for his courage.

Air raids and the constant tropical storms were the most significant problems the traveling USO shows faced. These brave people went through every possible discomfort and danger with their excruciating schedules. They performed in downpours and Japanese bombing raids and rode in aircraft into and out of military airstrips. They endured heat, insects, and, sometimes, mud up to their knees. They brought a piece of home to the fighting men, brightening their lives.

Many of those in the audience might be dead the next day. Some USO shows with Bob Hope and many other entertainment stars came to island installations throughout the Southwest Pacific, but unfortunately we were often working too far away to attend. Besides shows and movies, sports were extremely popular with the troops in their off-duty time. Many camps had baseball and basketball leagues. They built ball diamonds and basketball courts, with the help of Special Services.

The *Sea Horse* looked great in its new paint job. It was in the best shape—both inside and out—since coming off the ways at Fellows & Stewart. After George and Whitey finished tuning both engines and took the boat out for trials, I knew the moment I touched the throttle that it had new zip. I could feel the extra surge of power. The silky smoothness with no vibrations in the new shafts and propellers as it got up on plane was a tremendous feeling.

Now we were ready to go back to work.

15

On the Line

ON JULY 30, 1944, THE MONTH-LONG OPERATION TYPHOON commenced at the northwestern tip of New Guinea called the Vogelkop—or "bird head"—peninsula, in the middle of the sea and air routes between Asia, the East Indies, the Philippines, Australia, and New Zealand.

After the US occupation of Biak, Noemfoor, Sansapor, and Middleburg Island, they became bases for launching our air war on the Japanese in the Netherlands East Indies, Borneo, Halmahera, and the southern Philippines.

Sansapor was about 300 miles from the Netherlands East Indies, Halmahera, and Morotai, and only 750 miles from the southern tip of Mindanao. These new airfields shortened the distance our fighters and bombers had to fly to the Molucca Straits and part of the Celebes Islands. They also brought the eastern coast of Borneo's oil well and processing plants at Balikpapan within bombing range.

These new airfields at Sansapor and Middleburg islands were designated Mar Airdrome, after a small native village nearby.

Our new assignment was to cover Mar's flights by the 13th Fighter Command and the 13th Bomber Command. Later the 5th Air Force joined with the 13th Air Task Force, also named the Typhoon Task Force. They had battle-tested commanders, like Brigadier General Earl W. Barnes, 13th Fighter Command, and Typhoon Task Force Commander Major General Franklin C. Sibert.

The P-399 was covering the 347th Fighter Group (P-38 Lightnings), the 868th Bomber Squadron (B-24 Snoopers), and the 5th and 307th Bombardment Group. We also covered flights of the 18th Fighter Group and the 4th and 38th Photo Reconnaissance Squadrons, even though our orders didn't include them.

Our first day on duty at Sansapor and Middleburg Island, we were assigned to assist small landing craft (LCVPs and LCMs) encountering engine or operator problems by towing them out of the way of other vessels going to shore.

When we took up our station between the incoming troops, support vehicles, and supplies, we were shocked to find the *Sea Horse* caught up in the highest ground swells we had ever encountered. I judged them to be about ten feet tall at their peaks. There were no whitecaps and just a soft breeze.

The land swells caused the boat to leap to the crests and then drop suddenly into the troughs. A carnival ride wouldn't have given us a greater thrill. We had to keep the P-399 running so we could quarter the swells, and, after trying several times, we gave up anchoring because our anchor wouldn't hold.

During one of the landings, we were standing by, waiting for the ships offshore to begin lowering armament and equipment to "Ducks," the amphibious trucks, used to transport supplies to shore. Observing no activity, I took the *Sea Horse* closer to shore where we could see that the Japanese had fled their camps and retreated into the hills to escape the bombardment.

Jep asked permission to take a couple of the crew ashore to look around. I let them off at a dilapidated dock with strict orders to return within thirty minutes, or at a blast of the boat's horn. Barzow kept the binoculars on the front-line troopships to see whether they were dropping rope landing nets over the side, or ships' cranes were loading LCMs.

Unloading hadn't started. The crew didn't stay ashore long, and when they returned Jep said the Japanese had left in a big hurry because their cooking fires were still warm and rice cooking bowls were still sitting on the burned coconut husks.

While they were onshore, Bake and Ronnie hollered at Jep, "Hey, we're rich, we're rich!" Walking down to a palm hut, an office that housed the paymaster, he discovered that the Japanese had fled without taking their Netherlands East Indies invasion currency (junk guilder). There were also stacks of Philippine invasion pesos.

Ronnie and Baker carried three Japanese ammo boxes filled with the invasion currency back to the boat. I had seen a piece of it before as well as some ornate Tokyo Japanese currency. Although printed on flimsy paper, artwork on the bills was surprisingly good. The crew wanted to send some home, so Bake and Ronnie gave the crew a few notes and said that they would use the rest to trade for food with cooks and mess attendants on Liberty ships. We stored the currency in a locker.

Unloading the supply ships hadn't begun, due to the enormous land swells. Still, a little later command must have decided to risk losing cargo because they started bringing Ducks alongside the Liberty ships and lowering cargo in rope slings. Problems quickly arose from the swells, which brought the Ducks and the cranes up at the same time, causing the slings to dump some of their loads into the sea, where they floated off, up and down the high swells, with no one to retrieve them—except us. Some floated to where we were dragging anchor. It took only a moment for our crew to find themselves in the salvage business.

Ronnie and Baker tied half-inch lines around Jep and Whitey—our two best swimmers—under their Mae West life vests. Then they jumped into the heaving sea and swam to a floating cargo box. I maneuvered the *Sea Horse* over to them, and the crew pulled the crate aboard.

We continued until we had no more space on deck. We didn't keep many of the boxes containing items we could never use, but we kept a few containing trading materials. Bake and Ron were in scroungers' heaven. We opened boxes containing Lifesavers candy, scissors, barber equipment, wax candles, oil lamps, small buckets, and twine—all of which later proved to be aids when we visited villages.

When we put into a small island we took these "gifts from the sea" ashore to trade with islanders in return for information. They also promised to help and assist any downed airman landing in their waters.

Jep and Baker were in charge of the windfall loot.

16

Sansapor

On November 2 we arrived in northwest New Guinea to cover flights from Sansapor, Noemfoor, and Middleburg Island before moving to Morotai a week later. In August, Operation Typhoon secured the Allied operations area on the Vogelkop Peninsula from the Japanese.

With the Allies controlling the area, General Earl Barnes had a new airstrip built for his P-38 fighters. The air group would provide cover for the Morotai Task Force in a month and a half. He selected Middleburg Island near Cape Sansapor, and the Seabees and other engineering construction outfits went to work.

Clearing coconut trees and dense undergrowth from about 140 acres of the 240-acre island opened up land for a runway. Bulldozers moved nearly two hundred thousand cubic yards of jungle topsoil and sea coral to prepare a solid base. Large backhoes with tank treads dug more than forty-five thousand cubic yards of coral from the island's reefs at low tide.

After leveling the land with a heavy roller, they laid the final landing surface, more than five hundred thousand square feet of steel matting, to complete the base. This tremendous effort provided General Barnes's 13th Air Force Task Force and the 13th Fighter Command with an airstrip to carry the air war to hundreds of Japanese airfields, including the next big leap to Morotai, three hundred miles to the north.

By the time we arrived, the airfield was fully operational.

The P-399 covered the 42nd Bombardment Group B-25 flights from Mar, Noemfoor, Sansapor, and Middleburg Island. Flying cover to the

Celebes and Molucca Islands for these bombers were P-38s from the Eighteenth Fighter Group. Some of these roundtrip flights covered more than two thousand statute miles—the most extended fighter missions of the war.

The 347th Fighter Group was eager to operate from this new base—the most advanced in the Southwest Pacific. They faced the fierce defenses of Japanese planes and antiaircraft batteries; they had a severe flight problem because they couldn't stay over their targets long enough to conserve fuel for return trips to Klenso and Mar.

Belly tanks attached to P-38s increased fuel capacity but also cut down on the bomb and ammo capacity because of weight limitations. Many planes returned to Klenso with only a soda bottle full of petrol remaining in their tanks. Ground crews and mechanics sat on logs along the strip, sweating out the return of their pilots. Cheers erupted when their planes touched down.

The 13th Air Force Liberator bombers flew missions from Noemfoor to destroy one of Japan's most crucial wartime possessions: the oil wells and refinery at Balikpapan on the eastern coast of Borneo. Each bomber carried 3,500 gallons of high-octane gasoline (more than eleven tons). Strike planners had to reduce the amount of ammunition planes carried by half to stay within weight limits. Bomb loads were about 2,200 pounds. All of the fuel, ammo, and bombs brought the Liberators' load to about six tons, which was overweight.

To get their planes off the ground, pilots had to taxi to the end of the runway, lock their brakes, gun the engines to near maximum rpms, and, with full throttle, literally lift this burden slowly into the air. They cleared the end of the runway, with their retracting wheels about six feet above the water level at high tide, and, with a prayer, coaxed these huge, overloaded planes into the air.

We stood by holding our breath. Engines were laboring as the planes slowly gained altitude and then set their course, hoping to dump their bomb load on the target and return safely to base. This process continued, plane after plane, every ninety seconds until seventy-two Liberators were in flight formation headed for Balikpapan in the early morning darkness.

At the target Japanese ack-ack sprayed shells at them, and enemy fighters were constant threats to the unescorted Liberators. The fierce Japanese defenses didn't save Balikpapan. After five such raids by the 13th and 5th, the oil refinery and installation were no longer considered primary targets.

Although we were only on station at Sansapor for a brief time, we were glad to be on the flight line, doing air-sea rescue work—our primary mission. The crew was at its most productive, busiest, and satisfying level. They were happy to be in action, even though it was often life-threatening.

We experienced Japanese bombing raids by Betty and Judy aircraft, and we patrolled near the shores of occupied islands exposed to enemy gunfire. Baker said, "Their aim is so poor they couldn't hit a barn with a handful of rice." Charlie barges were formidable and we never challenged the thick-hulled vessels with their greater firepower.

Over the months our boat carried out many other assignments between patrols, such as carrying sick and wounded to station hospitals, moving threatened islanders from one island to another, and transporting medical and surgical supplies from back-base warehouses up to local surgical units.

One physician, a top-notch plastic surgeon whose practice was on Park Avenue in New York and charged ten thousand dollars per operation, offered me a free nose job after we had delivered their supplies so quickly. I was invited to their unit when they didn't have surgery scheduled, but I turned it down. Later, the recipient of two broken noses, I was sorry I hadn't accepted.

We took out command officers and engineers—the latter for offshore inspections—and welcomed convalescing and off-duty pilots who had a non-flying day to sail with us and, as they put it, "just to get off the rock." They relaxed. But no one after Guadalcanal tried to use the P-399 for recreational purposes. They were too busy fighting a war.

17

Morotai

On November 7 we arrived at Morotai, barely six weeks after the 31st Division, and the 126th Infantry Regiment, 32nd Division, had surged ashore, catching the small Japanese force by surprise and forcing their troops away from the southern coast. A secure perimeter defense protected the base against the Japanese.

Meanwhile the island was developing into a significant Allied base. Construction units immediately built airstrips to handle the 13th Air Force and Royal Australian Air Force aircraft. Two airfields were ready for use in October. Morotai played a vital role in liberating the Philippines during the remaining months in 1944 and 1945.

More and more units were moving three hundred miles north to the island, including the 38th Fighter Group. Our assignment was to cover the Pitu fighter strip and patrol the strait between Halmahera and Morotai. Our anchorage and dock were off the northwest corner of the airstrip, with facilities for unloading Liberty ships, but most ships came into the east side of the island off the Wama bomber strip. Johnny Cranston's P-406, another sixty-three-foot crash boat, was assigned to Wama Strip.

It was easier to cover flights to the north (Philippines) and west (Halmahera and Celebes), because of our proximity to the airstrip.

When we arrived, there were about thirty-seven thousand bypassed Japanese across the Morotai Strait on Halmahera, and approximately two thousand troops were cornered in the mountainous center section of Morotai by units from the 31st Infantry, which had a perimeter set up north of the airfields.

Japanese soldiers made several attempts to float on a log from Halmahera to central Morotai. Our orders were to stop any migration of these locked-in troops. PT boats also patrolled this area and were sinking enemy barges attempting to transport supplies to Morotai.

Morotai was reputedly the most bombed island in the Pacific. Air raids were almost continuous on some days and there were always two or three raids each night. Sometimes there were as many as five raids by Japanese Judys and Bettys attacking the airstrip at Pitu. Betty bombers, with their high-whining engines, also raided at night. Zero fighters came in low to strafe shipping in the harbor. Allied troops onshore and ground crew personnel had dug foxholes and covered them with coconut logs.

The *Sea Horse* tied up on the end of a long floating dock, or, if the docks were loaded, we anchored away from the pier. We watched the raids from our deck. There was no place to hide. We manned our twin-turret .50-caliber machine guns but had to be careful. We didn't want to hit another ship in the harbor. Morotai had an effective ack-ack defense and on most evenings our crew sat on the roof of the sickbay and watched the show.

Anticipating night raids from the Japanese, we sent up a couple of Black Widow night fighters who climbed to high altitudes and attacked the Bettys or Judys from above. One night the anti-aircraft guns were pumping away and just missed one of the night fighters. We had our short-wave radio on, and a voice yelled, "Hey, guys, knock off shooting at me! I'm on your side!"

A bomb falling a little close was unsettling. The power of those five-hundred-pounders exploding a couple of hundred yards away would scare anyone. You couldn't help but wonder if the next one might be right in your lap. The happy thought was that you would never know if it happened. But the Good Lord protected us.

The controllers in the Pitu tower were the best of any we had worked with at other bases. Together we completed many good rescues. The professional level of tower operators throughout the South Pacific was extremely high, but we seemed to hit it off with the Morotai operators. Mission times and courses were always on target, given to us early enough in the morning or sometimes late in the evening.

The first week at Morotai, while patrolling around the north end of Halmahera, we were given grid coordinates for the approximate location of a ditched B-24 Liberator. We wound up the *Sea Horse* and headed at full throttle for the coded grid area.

The P-399 could fly. We arrived at the spot, which was only a quarter of a mile off the shore of the island occupied with Japanese. We were within small-arms range from the coastline. The coastline was also an area where the Japanese hid their cleverly camouflaged barges during the day. You could look straight at them through binoculars and still not see them.

There was no air cover above the crash site to spot for us, so we had our binoculars trained on the calm sea searching for the downed aircraft. Finally, after we had sailed around the point of the island, Baker spotted the plane near a cove with the crewmen hanging on to the partially submerged fuselage and wings. We exposed ourselves to enemy fire, as we had no choice. These airmen had to be removed from the downed plane and soon.

We backed in alongside the plane and three aircrewmen jumped from the wreck and scrambled on board. The pilot, navigator, and gunner had all been injured when the plane hit the sea but had been able to get the hatch open and, with their Mae Wests inflated, had floated a short distance away from the wreck. The plane was about ready to sink, engine nacelles down first.

We lifted them aboard in the wire litter and carried them to the sickbay and the stern cockpit where Baker examined them and kept them covered while we dried their uniforms on the cockpit awning. All during the operation, I held my breath, expecting gunfire from the Japanese. We were sitting ducks, but luck was with us.

The *Sea Horse* headed for Pitu docks. Barzow called operations to request the base hospital have ambulances standing by when we docked.

They were there, along with a doctor and two nurses who took over from Baker. Each member of the Liberator crew thanked us before going ashore. We told them thanks weren't necessary. Like them, we were just doing our job.

Jep recorded each rescue by painting a hash mark next to a small parachute with a seahorse floating under it on the flying bridge's starboard side. Our numbers were rising. We surmounted lack of sleep, malaria, and the bad seas, which were frequent, to work together as a smooth, precision-working team. There were no typhoons or terrible storms during this period.

Because of the long flights north from Morotai to Japanese targets in the Philippines, and west to Borneo and Celebes, more and more planes suffered damage from enemy action. Fuel supply was a significant factor in their safe return to Morotai. Planes ditched and pilots bailed out.

A call came in one afternoon after a fighter pilot radioed a "mayday" to Pitu tower. They gave us the approximate grid coordinates. A choppy sea was running and visibility was marginal as we sailed to the estimated position of the ditched pilot. We began a "square search." Because visibility was poor, we set a course to the west, one-eighth mile, then traveled one-eighth mile south and the same distance due east.

In the search area, we only found a couple of floating coconuts. They looked like heads sticking out of the water, even when we were within fifty feet.

We extended our search to one-half mile, north, west, south, and east. We were trying to calculate the pilot's possible drift if he was in a one-person yellow life raft and extended our courses in that direction. On the third change of square search distances, Jep was up on the mast and spotted the pilot about one hundred yards off our starboard bow.

Barzow radioed Pitu tower with our ETA, so an ambulance and medic could be standing by on the dock. We sailed to the windward side of the pilot and the crew prepared the wire litter. Baker and Jep got in the water, lifted the man onto the litter, and hoisted him aboard. The flyer knelt, said a brief prayer, and thanked God for the Navy. We didn't tell him we weren't Navy. In his early twenties, the pilot was in shock after being tossed around in the sea for a couple of hours, thinking about shark attacks. In all of our seagoing times, we never heard of a shark-biting incident.

Baker took the young pilot, a major, down to the sickbay, gave him an ounce and a half of Old Taylor bourbon, removed his wet clothing, and wrapped him in a Navy blanket. We wasted no time in getting him back to base.

In a letter dated November 26, 1944, Jep wrote to Joyce about another rescue, "One of the fellows we picked up had been in the water sixteen hours and within a mile of [Japanese-] held islands ... when we got him aboard he fell to his knees and said a prayer. It made me feel very good ..."

Now and then, operations loaned us to other units. The Dutch East Indies needed a small gunboat to drop native scouts on Halmahera's northeast shore, which was occupied by some of the nineteen thousand Japanese troops bottled up on the island.

The drop point on Halmahera was about twenty-six miles from Pitu dock on Morotai. The mission was difficult because the scouts were being put ashore in early morning hours, requiring complete silence and secrecy—no lights, no sound. The Dutch briefed us on how to carry out the mission. Their interpreter went through the procedure with the scouts, who had done it many times before, for our benefit.

The scouts were small, young, and in tiptop condition. They were only about five-foot-two, an ideal size to move like shadows through the island's undergrowth, spying on the enemy.

Our departure time was 0300 hours. The moon phase was critical and planned by the Dutch for it to be favorable. Bright moonlight would have been disastrous. Each of the three scouts had a carefully prepared backpack, complete with a nylon strangling cord, and other support and protective items, including a big knife, but no gun. There was enough food to last them three days and nights. When they got ashore, their officer told us they would conceal themselves where they could watch the daytime military activity. At night they moved over the camp area and airstrip, returning to their hiding place during the day.

Our navigation had to be exact. In the darkness the shoreline loomed black and foreboding. I cut the port engine, but even with the starboard engine at near idle it still sounded like a rumble of thunder.

As we neared the drop point, the crew helped the scouts inflate their small, one-person rubber rafts. Bake was on the bow with our lead line, taking soundings and relaying the depths in a whisper to Whitey, who relayed them to Barzow and me. Ron was in the starboard gun turret in case the twin .50-caliber machine guns were needed.

When we were about fifty yards off the murky shore, about two fathoms over the coral bottom, we helped the scouts into their rafts and handed them their paddles. I held up three fingers and then pointed down, indicating we would be back in three early mornings. They nodded.

I looked at the shoreline and selected a spot with two trees that I was sure I would recognize on our return trip. We had a small flashlight to return their screened signal when we were ready to pick them up. They quickly melted into the darkness of the island night. George was going nuts about the big engine idling for so long, but I couldn't turn it off because it would roar when restarted.

I slowly backed the *Sea Horse* into deep water and swung around, moving at the lowest possible speed until we were out of hearing distance. Only then did George start the port engine, and I wound up the starboard engine. We covered the twenty or so miles back to our dock in quick order.

Coming into an anchorage or dock at night is always tricky. Everything looks different. Thank goodness the glow of a new day was brightening the east, but there was a groan from the crew when I told Jep we would get underway as usual for the morning flights.

I managed a two-hour nap before George started the engines. I woke up smelling the fresh-brewed coffee Ronnie was making in the galley, just outside the door of my quarters. Later, the weather was good and the sea quiet. I took time to swing by the shore where we had dropped off our native scouts.

Air raids were incessant. Every night the Japanese sent over at least one flight of bombers, and they often would come in low over Halmahera during the day to bomb the airstrips. Incoming afternoon flights could only land if the strips were damage-free. Otherwise they had to try and make it to Sansapor.

Over two months we sweated out more than one hundred raids, and the Japanese weren't dropping geisha pillows, either. We were all weary from the night work as well as the ups and downs of the night air raids. We weren't getting enough sleep.

Before we were due to pick up the native scouts, we ran into a little excitement.

Lieutenant Earl A. McCandlish and Salty AUTHORS' COLLECTION

Earl McCandlish's first command, the P-100, in her World War I configuration as a submarine chaser NATIONAL ARCHIVES

A bow shield attesting to the War Bond contributions of the citizens of Augusta, Kansas, is held in place on the bow of the P-399 by Miss Ellen Malcon (right) and Mrs. Jerry Steelright, on christening day, July 6, 1943. AUTHORS' COLLECTION

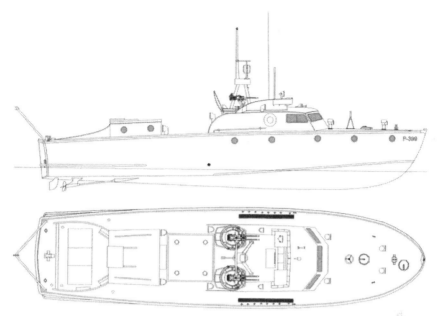

P-399 side elevation and deck plan AL ROSS II

The *Sea Horse* mate,
George L. ("Jep")
Jepson AUTHORS'
COLLECTION

Sea Horse flying off Halmahera Island AUTHORS' COLLECTION

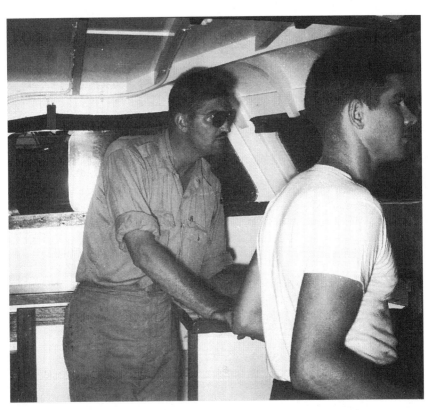

Earl McCandlish (left) and Jep in the pilot house AUTHORS' COLLECTION

Two AVR 63s similiar to the *Sea Horse*

ABOVE The P-399 crew in Wilmington, California, before personnel changes were made. Back (l-r) Jep with Salty, Earl McCandlish, Adam Taylor, and Hal Marshall. Front (l-r) Homer Baker, Ron Albrecht, Wilson Hollis, and Whitey Chaney BELOW Crew signatures and Salty's paw print on the back of the above photo AUTHORS' COLLECTION

Sea Horse, the best boat in the Pacific—a grand old gal AUTHORS' COLLECTION

Earl McCandlish ("Skipper") alongside the *Sea Horse* pilot house next to the image of a seahorse floating under a parachute and hash marks denoting rescues of downed pilots. Jep created the artwork.

The crew swam back from a village with a native dugout as an escort and climbed aboard. AUTHORS' COLLECTION

Baker (left), Jep (center), and Skipper bathing in a freshwater pool under a waterfall—a great treat—on a small island off Malabang, Mindanao
AUTHORS' COLLECTION

The *Sea Horse* crew at Morotai in March 1945 after Jep and Whitey received their Silver Stars and the others their Bronze Stars for the Galela Bay operation. Back (l-r) Homer Baker, Ron Albrecht, Earl McCandlish, George Savard, and George Jepson. Front (l-r) Reuben Barzow and Bill Chaney AUTHORS' COLLECTION

Good lad, Miguel, the young Filipino who came aboard at Zamboanga AUTHORS' COLLECTION

ABOVE *Sea Horse* (right) with a sister crash boat AUTHORS' COLLECTION
RIGHT Target practice with twin .50-caliber machine guns on the foredeck. Front (l-r) Reuben Barzow, George Jepson, Ron Albrecht, unidentified war correspondent. Background, Earl McCandlish AUTHORS' COLLECTION
BELOW A light moment in the South Seas, (l-r) Whitey Chaney, George L. Jepson, Earl McCandlish, and George Savard AUTHORS' COLLECTION

18

Battle of Galela Bay

On December 13, a beautiful tropical morning, four light-green P-40 Kittyhawk fighters from the Royal Australian Air Force 80 Squadron took off from Morotai on a routine mission to strafe Japanese positions on Halmahera across the Morotai Strait. As the squadron struck targets along Galela Bay, antiaircraft fire hit the plane flown by Flight Sergeant James Lennard.

At approximately 0905 hours, Lennard crash-landed his damaged aircraft on the beach a mile north of Galela Village. Severely injured, the twenty-year-old Aussie pilot took refuge under the left wing.

Thirty miles to the north, the *Sea Horse* cruised along on calm seas off Halmahera's north tip, a routine patrol. Some of the crew were still in their bunks catching up on sleep when our call letters crackled over the radio from Pitu Tower at 0935 hours. Responding to the base, we received the aircraft's approximate location.

The *Sea Horse* bolted ahead while Bake called general quarters, knowing the area bristled with Japanese troops and gun emplacements. All hands, a little bleary-eyed, were up and working at once. We closed on the plane's reported position in about forty minutes, preparing to go ashore in a rubber raft.

Jep was on watch, looking to spot the wreckage. Suddenly he turned to me on the bridge and said, "Skip, we've got trouble." The plane was lying about ten feet from the water's edge, right under Japanese guns.

As we neared the upper end of the beach at 1020, a Navy PBY circling the area started to land near shore, seemingly unaware of the heavy concentration of Japanese guns protecting the nearby Galela airstrip. As the plane was about to hit the water, the pilot gunned both engines and the Catalina climbed back into the air, alerted by Pitu Tower to the danger.

The RAAF pilot, who appeared to be injured, was visible under the wing, so I circled toward the beach. The Japanese opened up on us with 90-mm antiaircraft guns depressed to cover water approaches. Out of the corner of my eye, I could see tall geysers off our port beam. "Those aren't fish jumping," I yelled to Jep. I zigged and zagged but soon realized that the shots were going over our head as we neared shore. We were safe from the big guns as long as we were close to the beach.

Barzow called Pitu Tower and informed them we were outgunned and requested air cover while he provided Morotai with a play-by-play description as the battle developed. The tower responded that the 38th Air Group would cover us and "stand by," adding that the whole island was listening to Barzow's description of the radio attempt on the tower radio.

Within minutes, eight P-38 Lightnings from Pitu roared in, strafing the shore batteries and Japanese riflemen moving toward the beach. I spun the *Sea Horse* around and headed out to sea. It was apparent that approaching the beach in a rubber raft was impossible. So, Jep and Whitey, our two best swimmers, volunteered to swim ashore to bring the Aussie pilot back to the P-399. They put on their Mae Wests under blue shirts, an attempt to hide the yellow vests, and Baker tied a one-third-inch line around their waists.

Then we made a starboard strafing run on the trees and foliage behind the beach, after feinting a movement out to sea. Suddenly the unthinkable happened—our port engine conked out. I needed its reverse to keep us from washing up on a very unfriendly island. George was back on Morotai with an infected foot and our substitute engineer was of no help. About fifty yards from the beach we went aground in the sand. Jep and

Whitey dropped off the stern where they weren't visible to the Japanese and started for shore.

The P-38s continued low-level strafing runs while Bake, in one of the turrets, and Ronnie, on the bow, laid down withering fire with our twin .50-calibre machine guns. As Jep later wrote to his father, ". . . the boys on the boat were giving them hell. You should have seen the cook on the bow guns out in front of God and everybody . . . really pouring the lead."

Snipers targeted Jep and Whitey when they were only ten yards from the boat but they continued toward shore where they could see the pilot lying alongside the fuselage. Then all hell cut loose with heavy enemy fire, so we backed out of the sand, picked up Jep and Whitey, and retired to open water where the P-406 came alongside. Warrant Officer John Cranston and his engineer, Warrant Officer James Gray, climbed aboard the *Sea Horse*.

It was apparent the Japanese were using the pilot to decoy us into a trap. The fighters kept ground troops away from the RAAF plane while we called for Navy PTs to lay a smokescreen and bring additional firepower. By the time PTs 162 and 365 arrived, we had the port engine running again with assistance from Cranston and Gray, who helped keep the *Sea Horse* off the beach.

A new plan conceived in consultation with Pitu Tower and the PT skippers called for the PTs to launch smoke mortar shells onto the beach to shield the P-399 from the Japanese. PT 162 made a strafing run and drew heavy fire, while PT 365 stayed offshore with seven crewmen suffering with shrapnel wounds from enemy fire.

These PTs had been battle tested over many months, moving from the southern Slot up the island chain. In early August 1943, PT 162 was the boat closest to John F. Kennedy's PT 109 when it was rammed by the Japanese destroyer *Amagiri* in the Blackett Strait during an ill-conceived mission.

The smokescreen was successful, and the *Sea Horse* moved toward the beach, again going aground on a sandbar. Jep and Whitey went back in the water and swam toward shore. When they were within fifty yards of the beach, they observed that the tide had risen. The plane and pilot were nearly awash and there was no sign of life.

At the same time, the Japanese launched a mortar barrage. Jep and Whitey, growing weary, attempted to inflate their Mae Wests. Jep's worked, but Whitey's didn't, so they swam back sharing the good one. Once we pulled them back aboard we retreated across the danger line, averting enemy fire.

It was a sad and disappointing ending to the mission.

Barzow reported the situation to Pitu, and the P-38s returned to base. With only one fully functional engine, I requested that we return to base, which was approved. We were still eighteen miles or so from Morotai when a lumbering LCM, with a drop bow, was spotted coming toward us. Clinging to the metal grill on the drop gate was Lieutenant Colonel Wallace Ford, our squadron commander.

The *Sea Horse* eased alongside the LCM, and he clambered aboard. Ford said he had been listening to the Galela Bay battle, and it got so exciting that he decided to come over to see it, but his boat was too slow. The colonel congratulated everyone who had a part in the attempt to save the Australian pilot. When we finally tied up, I commended all hands for their courage under fire. Begging off mess, I went to my quarters, flopped on my bunk, and suddenly became extremely frightened, reflecting on the day's events.

The next morning George hobbled aboard, mad because he had missed the fun. A couple of weeks earlier he had stepped on a sea urchin and his foot had become infected. It only took him about fifteen minutes to identify what the trouble had been with our engine—the distributor rotor had cracked. He had a spare, and the Hall-Scott was soon purring like a kitten.

We fueled and arranged for John Cranston's P-406 to cover both Wama and Pitu airfields, allowing us to rest, re-arm, and make minor repairs to the hull.

Two days later, Jep wrote to his father: "I was wondering just how I would feel in combat, and I found out. I was scared as hell. And I don't think there was a man on the boat who didn't feel the same. We've got a damn good crew, and I would go through hell and high water with any man." He continued, "We were all talking last night about how lucky we were. And this morning, I found a bullet hole in one of the turrets. That was the only scratch we got. I also had to do my laundry if you know what I mean."

The same day, we cleaned our guns. There were about six inches of empty shell casings in the gun turrets.

Early the next morning, under cover of darkness, we picked up the scouts on Halmahera. We had little trouble finding the cove for the rendezvous. As we quietly coasted in, I had the queasy feeling that the Japanese had us in their sights and expected them to flash a spotlight on us. But there were just two little screened blinks from the scouts, which we returned, and soon we made out their dark shadows paddling out of the blackness. Once they came aboard, we roared out of there—mission accomplished.

On Christmas Eve, we received a call in the afternoon that a fighter was down in our sector. We headed out and followed our normal search procedures, eventually locating the general area where the plane ditched, but all we found was the pilot's parachute. It had been a rough few days for rescue attempts.

19

Baker's Red Hair

MOST OF OUR MISSIONS WERE WITHIN TWO TO THREE HOURS OF SAILING
time from Pitu, along the flight line toward the Molucca Straits, northwest of Morotai. We requested that the P-399 be permitted to anchor off
a small island named Rao, near the north end of Morotai. It was volcanic,
covered with palm trees, and had a small lagoon that provided shelter
from northeast winds.

We checked with the 31st Division Intelligence and our squadron
headquarters and learned there was a small Malaysian population on the
island. These people had initially migrated from Menado, Celebes Islands.
When the Japanese invaded there, they moved to Ternate off the west
coast of Halmahera and finally to Rao Island. About 150 people, including children, had banded together. Many of them were related. They had
moved from island to island in small boats.

These were cultured Malaysians living in a village called Leo-Leo.
Their leader was Philip Tambariki, who had been a schoolteacher on
Menado, Celebes, before the war disrupted their lives. They brought along
seed, chickens, and pigs; built homes; and created gardens. The island provided fruit, vegetables, and fish.

Overall they were living pretty well. The village even had a Singer
sewing machine (vintage 1930) with needles, shuttles, thread, and repair
parts. They appeared to be healthy, but most suffered from malaria. Some
of the children spoke excellent English.

The first evening we anchored in the lagoon, Philip Tambariki, his brother, and a friend came aboard to visit. He told us the latest history of his group and offered to teach us the Malaysian language. Jep, Barzow, and I accepted. Philip told us to get magazines such as *Life, Saturday Evening Post*, and others that we could obtain from Special Services so he could use the pictures to teach us the Malaysian name for items and objects.

His lessons helped us to better understand the islanders in the Malaysian areas. Our knowledge of his language, along with often-used phrases and greetings, was limited, but it came in handy, even in the extreme southern Philippine Islands, where some Malaysians lived.

After the day's patrol work was finished, Baker would keep busy visiting the village, where there were many malaria cases. He took a quinine and atabrine supply and often sat with individuals helping them through their high fever. He also treated and bandaged cuts.

The villagers loved Bake for his kind and professional way of caring for their sick children. They also loved his red hair and that he made them laugh, even though they had come through tough times.

Bake's red hair also created a problem. As we traveled throughout the South Pacific, the crew knew that women were attracted to his red hair, even to the point, in several cases, where their husbands asked if Bake would give their wives a redheaded baby.

These Malaysian villagers had close family units and were better educated than some of the islanders we had encountered. They didn't ask Bake for a redheaded child, but the attraction to his hair was noticeable. He always requested that Ron or Barzow accompany him to the village, riding shotgun just in case. Islanders' fascination with Baker's red hair began on one of the Solomon Islands when they would gather around him in awe.

In the Melanesian Islands—the Solomons, New Georgia, Bougainville, Treasury, and New Guinea—many men tried to dye their black hair red. It was a long and challenging procedure. They pulverized coral and seashells to make a paste, which they baked to produce a robust and caustic lime (calcium oxide). They mixed this with birdlime, juice extracted from ground up wild lime tree leaves, and lime juice. Working with a friend, they usually made enough paste for two heads.

As soon as the mixture was ready, they packed it on each other's hair, let it dry until it became hard as cement, and left it on their head for many weeks. When it came off, if all went well, there was a distinct reddish hue to their formerly jet-black hair.

Red hair made the wearer a significant person in village social life or the island's government. Eventually the red faded away, and it was necessary to repeat the process. New Guinea was the last island where I saw "lime heads."

Despite his red-hair problem, Bake was able to do many good things for the Malaysians, in the small amount of time available. Spending so much time in their homes, he spoke more of their language than Jep, Barzow, and me.

We shared fish with the village by chumming for them in the lagoon when the water churned with yellowfin, sea bass, small sword, and tuna. George would drop a grenade in the water and, presto, Leo-Leo, and the *Sea Horse* had a fish feast. Clawless Pacific lobsters were particularly tasty. In return, the villagers brought us fruit, eggs, and vegetables.

Sailing out of Rao Island a couple of times a week made duty easier because we didn't have to head out to the flight line so early. We got better sleep but were still awakened every night by bombing raids. It was easier to get supplies and gasoline when we docked at Pitu. It also allowed Baker to check the stateside Liberty ships that had just arrived, identified by brand new paint jobs, to see if he could trade for food.

One day Baker heard that two new ships were unloading on the east shore docks, trading targets for stateside food, and he asked me to drive him over. I had a borrowed jeep, so Bake, Ronnie, and I drove up the sand road along the north side of the Pitu airstrip.

We had driven about halfway around the strip when we spotted three Japanese soldiers walking out of a side path. When they saw us, they threw their arms in the air, and I pulled the jeep over to them. I unholstered my .45-caliber Colt pistol, and they went down on their knees, heads lowered. Baker and Ron motioned for them to get up. It seemed as though they thought we were going to cut their heads off, probably as their officers had warned them.

Baker pointed for them to head down the road. We walked them to the camp's stockade at the end of the strip, where guards took custody.

Along the way, guys came out of their huts, laughing as we passed. The Japanese were wearing US Army–issue shirts and pants, likely stolen off clotheslines on night trips into the camps foraging for food.

The Japanese soldiers were tired, I guess, of living in Morotai's interior jungle with no food and cruel, sadistic officers. They had probably decided to end it by surrendering to the evil Americans. I'm not sure, but I believe we were the only gunboat crew to capture three Japanese prisoners onshore, without firing a shot.

When we reached the island's east unloading docks, Baker told Ron and me to stay in the jeep while he went aboard the shiny, newly painted Liberty ship to trade for food with our Japanese invasion money. He had six bills. I reminded him we had three cartridge boxes full and asked why not give them a handful of the stuff in exchange for some meat. "If I take only a few with me, they'll think they're scarce, hard to get, and worth more," he said. "I'm only going to show them one to start."

Ron and I watched him go aboard. Shortly, he appeared on deck with someone in a white apron who looked to be a galley worker. They leaned over the rail and I could see Bake letting him sneak a peek at the "rare" Japanese invasion bill. They went inside and soon after, Bake returned to the jeep, all smiles. He told us about all the goodies he had procured for two of the Japanese bills.

The first bill was for the food. The second was to pay a Liberty ship crewman to get the four boxes of food off the ship and into the jeep without being detected. The boxes came off the ship so quickly I couldn't believe it. The galley hand put the four boxes in a large crate, took it over to the crane operator, and gave him the other Japanese bill. With that, he lowered our goods to the dock near our parked jeep.

The place was so busy with cargo coming off the ship that no one noticed our box. Ron and Baker put it in the jeep's rear, and off we went.

When we got back to the *Sea Horse*, we discovered that the boxes contained pure gold—frozen meat, including pork chops, hamburgers, bacon, and chicken, plus real potatoes, ketchup, mustard, mayonnaise, and a variety of canned vegetables. The crew was as happy as clams at high tide. Morale leaped 300 percent.

During the rest of our assignment at Morotai, Bake and Ron swapped Japanese junk invasion money for food, beer, and tobacco, sharing our newfound wealth whenever possible.

The Japanese had a lookout station and radio transmitter on the north end of Morotai that was tipping off their airfields and other targets whenever our planes took off on strikes. Morotai defense decided to close it down and sent in a company from the 31st Division. After they cleared the area, Signal Corps headquarters requested we take a few of their officers up to inspect the station.

They told us later that they were surprised at the high-tech equipment and were shocked when they found a primitive example of our transistor tube. The Allies believed this important technology was secret. The Japanese were not inventors, but master copiers, and had a well-devised spy network to steal inventions. Every Japanese Zero had an American Delco electrical system and many other parts manufactured using our processes.

On the return trip from the Japanese station, we brought a few seriously wounded Japanese and some of our casualties to the base hospital. One of the Japanese died on the way back. It took a long time to get the smell of death off the *Sea Horse*'s deck. The Japanese prisoners received the same medical attention as our men at the base.

While we were still at Morotai, we learned that the *Sea Horse* crew had been awarded medals by the War Department for bravery in action during the Galela Bay rescue attempt.

Colonel Ford had put this request through channels, with many endorsements, including the Royal Australian Air Force. The Far East Command liked our actions because it supported cooperation between countries and services in the Southwest Pacific. Of course, we did it because that was our mission, regardless of under which flag pilots flew.

When asked to submit a list of our crew present at Galela Bay, I added John Cranston and James Gray. Each had taken a significant risk in coming aboard to assist us on deck and in the engine room while we had two men in the water.

Jep and Whitey were awarded the Silver Star for "gallantry in action." Baker, Ronnie, Barzow, Cranston, Gray, and I received the Bronze Star for "meritorious achievement."

On the day of the award ceremony in March 1945, I went into shock when the crew informed me they didn't have starched parade clothes or shoes. They didn't have shoes because regular-issue footwear, made with heavy leather, wasn't fit for deck use. We had requested canvas deck shoes, but supply turned us down. When the crew received the leather shoes, they cut the tops off, leaving the bottom and a small strap across the instep. The shoes were cooler but didn't qualify for an inspection by an Air Force general and his staff.

I told them to request new shoes, shirts, and pants from supply. Failing this, they had to borrow shoes from the ground crews at Pitu airstrip. Lacking new shirts and pants, they were to take their own to the hospital laundry for a quick ironing job. Bake issued Japanese invasion money to grease palms at supply, shoe borrowing, and the laundry.

They were all back in a few hours, all set with everything but insignia. Sewing stripes and unit patches on their shirts slipped our minds. So they wielded needles and thread like crazy. A quick inspection showed they could get through an hour-long ceremony if the command didn't look too closely. Ronnie and Chaney were in a lot of pain because their borrowed shoes were too small. They went barefoot and carried the shoes until we fell in for the awards.

I enjoyed hearing praise from my peers for the P-399 and its crew. It was a day to be remembered.

On December 7, 1991, fifty years after the Japanese sneak attack on Pearl Harbor, I called members of the *Sea Horse* crew and pledged to wear the Bronze Star lapel pin on my jacket in their memory.

While we were still at Morotai in the Netherlands East Indies, bombing raids on the Japanese positions in the Philippines continued to increase. We were a lot busier responding to distress calls from pilots.

Early one morning before dawn we received a report that a fighter pilot had crash-landed forty miles from shore. Already on the flight line, we started our search pattern and three hours later we located the airman in his small rubber raft. He was nibbling on a cracker and reading his handbook *How to Survive in the Jungle.*

This kid was one relaxed flyer, shading himself from the sun with his parachute while he held his handbook with one hand and wielded a fishing pole in the other. If we hadn't arrived so soon he would have been just fine. He was all set with provisions—two canteens of water, rations, a medical kit, signal equipment, a compass, revolver, and Dutch currency.

"I've been expecting you fellows," he yelled, "but you're just too late for breakfast." Climbing aboard the *Sea Horse* with a smile, he remarked, "I don't suppose anyone remembered to bring my mail."

On another routine patrol, this time with an AAF news reporter and the cook from a visiting ocean liner as our guests, we picked up a fighter pilot returning from a raid in the Philippines who crash-landed in our sector.

As we returned to base, the cook was panic-stricken when he realized his ship had embarked for the US, leaving him behind. Not so funny for him were the keys to the captain's pantry clinking in his pocket. The cook had permission to accompany us on patrol, but his ship sailed unexpectedly. Attempts to contact the P-399 by radio had failed.

So we chased after the ship, which had a two-hour head start. The *Sea Horse* climbed up on plane and we caught up with the liner, which stopped and lowered a rope ladder to our deck. The cook climbed upward to catcalls from his shipmates lining the rail and the severe glare from his captain.

An officer on the bridge with a bullhorn, speaking slowly, said, "Thank you *Sea Horse* for your delivery service. The next time you borrow the captain's cook, consider him a gift."

Fighters seemed to be regularly dropping into the sea between Morotai and the Philippines. Another day we received a distress call that a pilot was ditching about forty miles from our present position.

Three hours later we spotted a life raft and the pilot. Tears ran down his face as he stepped aboard the *Sea Horse*. "When I saw you coming, I got down on my knees and thanked God for the Navy," he blurted.

Jep shook hands with the young flyer and said, "Lieutenant, add a P.S. to your prayer and say a good word for present company, this is an Army boat and crew."

Embarrassed and blushing, the pilot replied, "Did I pull a boner, if *I* were you, I'd toss me back to the fishes."

20

Task Group 78.2

<small>By April 1945 the war had moved north into the Philippines.</small> General MacArthur made good his promise to the Philippine people on October 20, 1944, wading ashore on Leyte Island after his troops had landed. "People of the Philippines, I have returned!" he declared in a radio broadcast.

In January 1945 MacArthur's forces landed on Luzon, the main Philippine island. A month later Corregidor was recaptured and Japanese forces on Bataan were isolated. Manila, the Philippine capital, toppled in March. Sadly just one-third of the men left behind when MacArthur was evacuated to Australia in 1942 had survived the war.

"I'm a little late," he said, "but we finally came."

With fewer bombing raids flown out of Wama Drome, Morotai, we weighed anchor at Rao Island and returned to operate full-time out of Pitu.

The last night at Rao we all went ashore for a farewell party. Baker and Ronnie brought three large cakes from the enlisted men's mess on Morotai (using some of the Japanese invasion money), which was a tremendous treat for our Malaysian friends. As we were leaving we exchanged addresses with Philip Tambariki and his friends and swore we would write after the war. We never did write, but that was the nature of wartime promises.

Our crew, particularly Bake, had made good friends of these people. They were just like families around the world, no matter how remote—a mother with a sick child, a child without the support of a parent, a father with a hungry family. Families everywhere face life much the same.

The next morning we were out on the flight line at sunrise and never saw Rao again. Our work continued as before, until one day, out of a clear, blue sky, while we were on patrol off north Halmahera, operations radioed a coded order moving us at once. I was stunned because I hadn't made provisions for a change of station. We were low on water, gas, and food.

The order directed the P-399 to overtake Amphibious Task Group 78.2, which was bound for Mindanao in the Southern Philippines with the 24th Infantry Division and Headquarters X Corps under Major General R. B. Woodruff, Major General F. C. Sibert, and Vice Admiral A. G. Noble. General MacArthur's orders were to clear Japanese troops from the island.

The operation wasn't necessary because the forty-three thousand enemy soldiers had been bypassed, contained by twenty-five thousand guerrillas under Colonel Wendell Fertig, a former civilian mining engineer. The guerrillas controlled about 95 percent of the island. There was no valid military reason for a large, powerful invasion force to hit Mindanao. It was merely an action undertaken to fulfill MacArthur's promise and please our Philippine friends (and the Moros, who hated the Japanese).

"I shall return," MacArthur had said. And he did.

TG 78.2 sailed south from the central island of Mindoro. It looped around the Zamboanga Peninsula where the second part of the invasion force, the 31st Infantry Division from Morotai, under General C. A. Martin, joined it.

TG 78.2's destination was Malabang, Parang, and Cotobato, on the west shore of Davao Peninsula on the Moro Gulf, Mindanao Island. The invasion force left Mindoro on April 11, 1945. We weren't aware of it because it sailed under blackout and the 31st Division loaded on Landing Ship Infantries (LSIs) and Landing Ship Tanks (LSTs) on the east shore of Morotai. As a result, we didn't see it sail north so we were surprised to be ordered to join TG 78.2.

I called the crew together and explained what I knew. I said all we could do was follow orders, overtake the task group, tie up to a larger ship, and hitch a ride to Mindanao.

The *Sea Horse* could fly, and with it kicking up a rooster tail it didn't take us long to spot ships in the task group on the horizon. Approaching the trailing vessels, I maneuvered the P-399 alongside an LSI, which permitted us to tie up to their stern. They threw us a light cable and George cut the engines. Ron prepared a meal, and we stretched out and relaxed.

It didn't last long. Barzow received relayed flag code signal for the P-399 to report to Rear Admiral Noble's flagship, USS *Wasatch*, a Mount McKinley–class amphibious command ship. General Sibert of the 31st Division and General Woodruff of the 24th Division were also aboard. They had a decision to make.

On the day of TG 78.2's departure from Mindoro, they received an intelligence report that the Mindanao guerrillas, under Colonel Fertig, had cleared the town and airstrip at Malabang of Japanese. The area was now under their control. Since April 3, Colonel Clayton C. Jerome's Marine Air Group Zamboanga (MAGSZAM), flying SBD Dauntless dive bombers and F4U Corsair fighters, had launched air strikes against Japanese positions from the Malabang airstrip.

When this news reached Generals Sibert and Woodruff aboard the *Wasatch*, and General Eichelberger on the cruiser *Montpelier* with Admiral Riggs, a decision was made to change the invasion plan under strict radio, signal, and visual security. While the fleet was en route to the invasion objective new orders were prepared for distribution to the task group.

Wasatch signaled us to come alongside. I spoke with George and Jep, telling them I didn't know what to expect but that we would do our best. George wasn't sure we had enough gasoline to carry out an extended duty but said he and Whitey would monitor both tanks' fuel levels.

Jep removed the LCI's cable and yelled to the seaman on the deck that we would be back. My first job was to find the *Wasatch* among the waves of ships. It was still light enough to read masthead signal flags, and Barzow made sure he knew what a commodore's flag looked like so we could pick it out at the van of TG 78.2. The *Sea Horse* weaved through the task group to the *Wasatch*, which Barzow and Jep picked out of three large ships near the van.

On the way we made emergency preparations. Should we start to run out of gas, two lines were ready to throw to the nearest ship. Blackout curtains on the main bridge maintained the security blackout should light for reading maps or charts be required. The companionway hatch was to remain closed.

I eased the *Sea Horse* up on the *Wasatch's* starboard beam. We were about twenty feet away but we could feel the wake. A staff officer yelled to us through a bullhorn, maintaining radio silence and a light signal blackout. With a heaving line, he tossed down a leather shaving kit, a separate packet with our orders, and another box containing maps. The orders specified directions for delivering orders to ships in the task group and included a map showing each ship's location in the task group.

The deck officer shouted, "Good luck, Sailors!"

"We're going to need it," I muttered to myself.

Looking at the sixty-plus ships making up TG 78.2, I realized this was one hell of a job. A multi-million-dollar, combined-services invasion defended by over forty-three thousand Japanese troops was ahead of us, and an air-sea rescue gunboat was delivering the plan to liberate it with a shaving kit.

Jep had several heaving lines with monkey fists onboard should we lose the one tied to the kit. I maneuvered the *Sea Horse* to the eastside of the fleet, where destroyers were protecting the cargo and troop ships from the Japanese submarines they believed were trailing us. I carefully read the instructions and studied each ship's location in the task group.

There was no way I could memorize the names and positions of so many ships. We would have to do this one at a time. We would locate a ship on our list, then deliver the orders while Barzow prepared the next ship's name and location.

I wondered what the hell would have happened if we had not been available at Morotai to deliver the command's change of orders to TG

78.2. Why was an AAF air-sea rescue boat, rather than a Navy gunboat or PT, ordered to perform this crucial mission on which the orderly invasion of Mindanao depended? We were flattered that command, which had assigned the task to the P-399, had confidence in our ability to perform. Maybe it was our Galela Bay record.

The destroyer USS *Flusser* was close by, so we approached its starboard beam. Jep put their new orders in the shaving kit and tossed the heaving line to an officer on the deck. He removed the orders and threw the bag back to our foredeck—so far, so good. Baker successfully heaved package two to the second ship and retrieved the line. Ron took a try at it and did fine.

We moved from vessel to vessel—LCIs, cruisers, destroyer escorts, and the US Coast Guard Cutter *Spencer* with General Eichelberger onboard. Admiral Noble later moved his flag from the *Wasatch* to the *Spencer* for the offshore fighting in Davao Bay. Finding a Coast Guard ship that America equated with protecting our vast coastlines in a battle zone was surprising. But it probably was just as eye-opening to the *Spencer* to find an AAF air-sea rescue gunboat working the night shift for TG 78.2 between Morotai and Parang, Mindanao.

Working in and around the fleet was not too difficult during the late afternoon hours, but this changed after dark when large ships loomed out of nowhere and appeared too tall for us to reach with a heaving line. There were a few misses with the monkey fist and we had to toss it again, but the crew kept at it.

Pale light heralded a welcome beginning to dawn. As visibility increased, we took short cuts around ships, often barely missing their intimidating bows. The helmsmen aboard these vessels must have cussed us out. I was glad there were no carriers or battleships in the fleet. I don't think the crew's pitching arms could have tossed a heaving line that high.

Carriers were not needed in this invasion because Colonel Jerome's MAGSZAM had swept the skies of Japanese aircraft on Mindanao.

There were reports that the Japanese lacked pilots, and their maintenance and repair crews couldn't keep their planes in the air. They had pulled back their best air squadrons from Indonesia and the southern Philippines to protect Japan. Command knew that the 347th P-38s stationed at Morotai could provide support if needed.

Our last delivery was to Lieutenant Colonel Robert Amory, who commanded the Army's 533rd Engineer Boat and Shore Regiment landing craft flotilla. After the war, Amory served as Deputy Director of the Central Intelligence Agency from 1952 to 1962. The amphibians would go ashore in waves after the naval bombardment known as a "Spruance Haircut."

Spruance Haircuts were so named because of the appearance of coconut groves after the palm fronds at the top of each tree trunk were scissored off by five- and eight-inch guns from Admiral Raymond Spruance's cruisers during the pre-invasion bombardment of an island's shoreline. The accuracy of the ships' guns from miles at sea was incredible. They aimed at this level to hit installations and airfields built inland, away from the coconut groves along the shore. The frondless tree trunks sticking up at the same level resembled a crewcut when viewed from the sea.

I asked George if we had enough gas to report to the *Wasatch*. He said it would be close, but we could try. If we ran out maybe we could hitch a tow from our old friend Lieutenant Bob Pickering, commander of a squadron of 110-foot gunboats (PGM's). Bob was the skipper of the PGM-4, which had accompanied the *Sea Horse* south from the Treasury Islands to Kiriwina Island in a raging typhoon earlier in our South Pacific duty. During our deliveries we had pulled alongside PGM-4, but it didn't ring a bell until we finished. It would have been good to wave to him.

Low on gas and with a tired crew we pulled up to the *Wasatch*. I yelled to the deck officer to tell the commodore that we had delivered orders to the entire task group. Jep threw back their "10-million-dollar" shaving kit and we sailed back to our tow, the LCI. Just as we grabbed the cable, the engines coughed and sputtered like we needed gas.

I told the crew I was proud of their work assisting in the joint command's gamble. Jep set single watches until the task group reached Parang. I went below but don't remember falling into my bunk; I was exhausted.

It was April 17 and it seemed as if I had barely dozed off when Barzow, who had the morning deck watch, woke me and said that Vice-Admiral Riggs' cruisers and destroyers were sailing into position to bombard Parang and Cotabato. Jep had somehow gotten us tied up to a small supply ship loaded with Corps of Engineers material for bridges. Thankfully we were a long way from the shoreline and the rolling thunder of the big guns.

Assault waves landed on their assigned beaches without opposition and moved steadily inland. In the days ahead, gunboats commanded by Lieutenant Bob Pickering and Captain Rae Arison supported troops going up the treacherous Mindanao River.

Using our intercom-radio, George and Barzow located a high-octane gasoline barge attached to PT Squadron 24, and we made the short distance to it. George said he was amazed that we had a few drops left to get there. We took on all they would give us at that time, about two hundred gallons. While we were pumping gas, with the red "Baker" flag on the yardarm, Barzow relayed a radio message from the commodore, requesting P-399's skipper to come aboard the flagship.

As soon as we completed refueling, we approached the *Wasatch* and requested permission to come aboard. Jep and George came with me. Admiral Noble gave us a hearty welcome and we saluted in our best military manner, something with which we had little practice. He and his executive officer were cordial and flattering about our successful mission, but there was no written commendation to my commander, Colonel Ford.

The exec asked if we needed anything. I explained that we had left Morotai without prior notice and didn't have time to refuel or secure food, supplies, and water. I told him we already owed a chit for two hundred gallons of 110-octane fuel. The admiral ordered his supply officer to write the necessary chits for us. I put the three separate orders in my shirt pocket, thanked them, saluted the ensign, and left.

After circulating through the supply ships, we found the one listed on our chit. I went aboard and spoke with the officer of the day, who directed me to the issuing officer. I gave him our chit, and he looked at me, taking in our AAF insignia and my crushed cap, shrugged, and said, "Where do you want us to put this?"

I pointed to the starboard side and we walked over to the rail. Looking down on the P-399, he started to laugh, really laugh. Supply officers didn't usually laugh. Then he said, "The commodore gave you a chit for a destroyer escort ration supply, which weighs several tons. If I gave you all of this we'd sink your boat, but maybe we can work something out."

The Navy can always work something out and did. The supply officer gave me the fleet number of a ship that would take aboard the entire ration issue and then dole out what we needed, including meat, fresh vegetables, coffee, tobacco, and 3.2 beer. He said that he had watched us deliver orders the night before and was glad to help us.

Later that afternoon, the destroyer escort's skipper gave us our share and there was a grand celebration aboard. But I didn't think we could sail with the boxes and crates stacked all over the deck. We could only take a small amount of frozen meat because of our small refrigerator. The destroyer escort allowed us to come by each day while we were at Parang and pick up what we needed.

The shorefront at Prabang took on a fresh look, with newly repaired docks. The unloading of materials and personnel continued. Trucks, tanks, and troops moved across the island up the Mindanao River, following the first wave.

We lost track of the Davao inland war when we received orders to support Colonel Jerome's MAGSZAM, which had been flying out of Malabang airstrip since April 3 after guerrillas cleared the area of Japanese. We reported to Colonel Jerome at about the same time the 24th Marine Air Group F4U Corsairs flew into Malabang to provide close air support for the Army action around Davao and against the forty-five thousand Japanese troops cut off inland.

The crew wondered what this would mean for us.

The Philippines

THE SAIL ALONG THE MINDANAO COAST FROM PARANG-COTABATO TO Malabang was smooth and relaxing. The second-largest island in the Philippines was also one of the most rugged. It had a dense forest of mahogany, banyan, sandalwood, and, on the coast, cypress trees. The lumber business was its most important industry, next to the manufacture of sisal rope.

Inland there were marsh and grass areas, and many lakes, especially Lake Lanao in the north-central part of the island. Its coast is typical of the Philippines, with small towns and villages where coves provided good anchorages.

Mindanao has a strange shape, with three peninsulas in the southern part, one tipped by Zamboanga on the southwest and twin capes bordering Davao Bay. The vast, island-dotted expanse of the Moro Gulf lies between Zamboanga and Davao.

The population on most of the southern islands included Spanish-speaking Filipinos and Asiatic Muslim descendants called Moros. There had been, and still is, an extremely hostile relationship between the two, with many local wars and conflicts, mostly religious but some over land possession and living standards. A third group in the population, Melanesian Negroid people, lived in the inland mountainous regions.

As we made landfall at Malabang, Barzow reported in and told them we were standing by, monitoring the flight operations radio channel. I officially reported to MAGSZAM headquarters the following morning.

Three beaches designated during planning for the invasion were available: Red, White, and Blue. We chose to anchor off Blue Beach. The downside of this decision was that it was much farther away from the airstrip, but the advantage was that it was mostly sheltered from the weather by a small, fertile, palm-covered island, with freshwater streams.

This island had a small village and we could hear the voices of the children at play from our anchorage. We made two attempts to anchor because the coral bottom kept breaking off. I planned to request an old aircraft engine to drop at our anchorage so we could fashion a makeshift mooring buoy.

The next morning Jep dropped me off at the small Malabang dock. We didn't tie up because it was busy and crowded with fast supply vessels. I located headquarters and reported, feeling the amicable atmosphere compared to the other installations where we had worked. These Marines were friendly and extremely helpful.

After leaving Colonel Jerome's office, I arranged for supplies. The Marine air group ground crew told me where to contact the tankers that would come down to the Malabang dock to refuel us. Not surprising, vehicles were difficult to come by, which meant walking from Blue Beach to camp if we were at anchor—a distance of half a mile.

I walked the jungle path along the shore from Red Beach to Blue Beach to check it out. It was very primitive. Even in the middle of the day, covered with a leaf-and-vine awning, it was shadowed and hot. You could sweat a quart just standing there. Finally, I reached Blue Beach and stood on the shore waving to the P-399, which was anchored fifty yards out. After a time, the watch saw me, and Jep came for me in our black, rubber raft with an outboard motor.

"What was the crew doing up on the bridge?" I asked Jep. He said the watch didn't see me at first because they were busy watching village families taking their daily bath in the freshwater stream flowing into the sea, opposite to our anchorage. "Watching people take baths?" I asked. Staying silent, he brought the tender into our boarding net. By the time I came aboard, everyone had dispersed.

During mess, Jep said he wanted to check out the freshwater stream above the village laundry and bathing area where the crew could enjoy freshwater baths. The next afternoon, after patrol, Jep and Barzow took the tender over to the small offshore island to investigate the river gushing into the tidewater about a hundred yards from the nearest hut.

The two of them were gone about half an hour and returned with a report about the swimming and bathing pool with a thirty-foot waterfall pouring into it. Jep set up a lottery to determine who would be the first to enjoy this welcome treat.

Villagers bathed at the mouth of the stream, pouring water over their heads and bodies using half of a dried coconut shell. Village men, except for the elderly, bathed early in the morning. Women and children bathed the rest of the day. Most brought their laundry, washing in the brackish water at the stream outlet and beating it on large stones worn smooth after hundreds of years of use.

We were off patrol the following day. Leaving Bill Chaney on watch, the rest of us went ashore with towels and soap. It was a lovely tropical spot. Tall coconut palms surrounded the glen on two sides of the pool and a beautiful, splashing waterfall on the inland side. A rim along each side of the top of the fall went back to a slope of tree-covered hills.

In minutes, we jumped into the crystal clear, crisp, fresh water. After a bath and a swim, I was toweling off when we heard a woman laugh. All of our eyes looked up, searching the rim along the falls. So help me, the entire village was peering down on us. As we were nude, instinct caused us to jump back in the pool, but the funniest sight was Baker trying to hide behind a young tree, with a trunk the size of one-inch manila line.

The villagers laughed and enjoyed looking at us, perhaps because of our bare white skin, which contrasted with our deep tans. Once again, we dried off and dressed. As we prepared to return to the P-399, a few villagers came down and asked for our soap. I nodded, and the crew gave them the bars we had with us.

They were friendly Moros. Both the women and men surrounded Baker. Not surprisingly, they liked his ginger hair. As we were leaving, they gave our raft a friendly shove. When we returned to the *Sea Horse*, Ron, Barzow, and Baker took Whitey over for his turn under the falls.

Security at operations told me to make sure we had an adequate watch on deck. This precaution was to protect against the possibility of a Moro activist attempting to come aboard to get our machine guns and ammo and small arms. I took the advice seriously. While on watch, we had observed *proas* (outrigger canoes) with six paddlers and a couple of riders crossing from Mindanao to our small island late at night. The crew was concerned and we doubled the watch, with two men armed with pistols on night and day.

Marine Corsair and Dauntless pilots reputedly exhibited an absolute lack of fear of crashing, facing Japanese aircraft or ground defenses, ditching at sea, parachuting into jungles, or even their commanders, who, in most cases, were just like them.

I'm not deprecating the bravery of Air Corps or Navy pilots. They were no less brave or skilled as flyers. But the Marine pilot was different.

We connect the time-honored name "marine" with mud-sloshing, mosquito-fighting, jungle-crawling, knife-wielding rifle marksmen. But we seldom link Marines with their exploits in air combat where Colonel Jerome's MAGSZAM excelled. It was an honor to work with them.

Our mission was somewhat easier because most of the Marine flight patterns were over the island's interior. Fewer strikes occurred over Moro Gulf and Davao Bay. Japanese naval activity now amounted to a few hidden barges that only ventured out at night to contact Japanese troops who had been bypassed and trapped on islands.

MAGSZAM supported the ground war around Davao and along Highway 1 and the Sayre Highway from Davao City to Cagayan de Oro and down to Sarangani Bay in the south.

The Japanese were adept at camouflaging, so finding their camps in the jungle and mountains was extremely difficult. Pinpointing them for aerial attacks required dangerous treetop flying at speeds up to three hundred miles per hour. The skill of these pilots amazed us.

As they were returning to base they would often dive and buzz the *Sea Horse*. We shuddered when we spotted them coming down. It seemed they were never going to pull up, but they did. What worried us most was that they wouldn't know our radio antenna extended above our mast by eight feet or more. I called them on our intercom, explaining my concern, but they only laughed and said not to worry.

The pilots' blue language on the intercom was unbelievable. Headquarters always censored them for "dirty language" spoken during the serious business of giving their positions and targets, often accompanied by high-spirited banter and friendly insults. Barzow, frequently listening, was always laughing. I wonder what the Japanese, who tuned in to our channels, thought of MAGSZAM communications.

When the guerrillas cleared Malabang Village and the airstrip, the Marines set up a secure perimeter with guard posts every thirty or forty feet to keep out infiltrating Japanese looking for food and clothing. Real trouble developed when Moros would sneak into the marine camp like shadows in the night while the Marines were sleeping, slip into their tents, and steal guns and ammunition. They needed weapons for their constant fight with the Filipinos.

Losing weapons was terrible, but a minor consideration if a Marine awakened and the Moro killed him. After the fifth or sixth such killing, Colonel Jerome tripled the perimeter guard and ordered them to capture, but not kill, the next invading Moros. After a week the guards seized three Moro fanatics inside the compound. Colonel Jerome had the guerrillas catch three wild pigs in the hills near the camp and bring the whole hides to him.

The following Saturday, when the colonel knew most Moros would be in their villages along Lake Lanao, he and his staff took the Moro prisoners in jeeps to Bayang. Wrapping the screaming, clawing, and twisting prisoners in pigskins and binding them securely, the Marines dragged them through the village. The Moro revulsion at coming in contact with pigskin was so great that there were no more sneak attacks on the Marine base.

22

VE Day

On May 8, 1945, returning to our anchorage at Blue Beach, we tied up and shut down the intercom radio from a routine patrol. Barzow flipped on our big liaison radio, with worldwide reception, and yelled, "Hey, the war's over in Europe!"

We all gathered around Barzow's radio and listened to broadcasts of the momentous VE Day story, including President Harry Truman's address to the American people announcing Germany's unconditional surrender. The president made no mention of a celebration, cautioning that, "Our victory is but half-won. The west is free, but the east is still in bondage to the treacherous tyranny of the Japanese. When the last Japanese division has surrendered unconditionally, then only will our fighting job be done."

With the battles still raging closer to the Japanese islands, we knew there was still work to be done in the Pacific, but Germany's surrender brought uplifting thoughts of the war against Japan ending.

Despite the president's somber tone, celebrations from around the world, particularly from Great Britain and Europe, poured from Barzow's speaker. We looked at each other. Savard looked at me.

"Skipper, it seems like everyone is celebrating VE Day, but us."

"Sorry, but the Three Feathers whiskey has been gone for a few months, and the corner liquor store is closed."

After a moment's pause, I asked Jep to strap on his .45 pistol.

"We'll go up to the base to see if we can find some booze at the Pilot's Club," I announced.

Jep and Baker lowered the outboard tender overboard, and we took it into Blue Beach and pulled it far up on the shore. We always hoped that an islander, especially a Moro, wouldn't steal it. Our watch aboard the *Sea Horse* periodically trained binoculars on it when someone was ashore.

We trudged up the jungle path toward the base, with spiny iguanas waddling across the sand road in several places. They were just as unhappy to confront us as we were them. They were big, and they were ugly.

When we arrived at the base, I had an idea. "Let's go over to the colonel's shack," I suggested. "Maybe he's having a VE Day party."

When we got there, all was quiet—no party. I knocked on the screen door, and there was no response. Just as we were leaving, the entrance to the Dale Hut next door opened and a Marine major came over to inquire if we were looking for Colonel Jerome.

We told him we had just heard the news about VE Day and had come to see if we could borrow some whiskey from the colonel to celebrate. The major said the colonel had flown up to Leyte to celebrate there. And then he said, "Come on in the colonel's digs, we'll look for his liquor supply."

Entering the hut, the major pulled a footlocker from the corner and opened it up. Wow! Canadian Club, Johnny Walker Scotch, and Vickers Gin abounded.

"Lieutenant, how many men do you have in your crew?" he asked.

"Major, I haven't counted lately, but I think fifty," I responded, with a straight face.

"Fifty! Is that your boat, that pint-sized rowboat I see in Illana Bay doing patrol?"

I admitted that perhaps our crew was not quite that big, but we would take as many bottles as we could get. The major gave us four, and kept two for himself, closed the locker, and slid it back in the corner.

Stepping outside the colonel's hut, we thanked the major for his generosity. It was beginning to get dark so we headed for the base motor pool to hitch a ride back to Blue Beach. Neither of us wanted to hike back in the dark.

We each put two bottles inside our shirts, where we could fold our arms over them. There was a Marine corporal on duty, while the sergeant, already absent for two hours, finished his evening mess. The corporal said we could have a ride when the sergeant authorized it and could get someone to drive us down. While we waited, he spotted the bottles in my shirt and asked for a drink. I gave him a slug of gin.

Finally the sergeant returned and we requested a ride. "Okay, but I'll need some of that booze—now," he said.

He had a drink, sent the corporal to get a driver for us, and had another drink. When the jeep pulled up, the sergeant, the corporal, and the driver each had a drink, so I left the bottle. It was against military regulations to have an alcoholic beverage in your quarters or aboard your ship, except GI-issue beer, without special permission from your commander—a rule rarely enforced.

We drove toward Blue Beach, but near the edge of camp the driver said he was still thirsty and that a drink would help the jeep moving toward Blue Beach. So Jep pulled out one of his bottles and let the driver take a big swallow. Reaching the beach, he said he would need a few drinks to get back to base, and if we needed a jeep in the future to come and see him or the sergeant and they would take care of us. It seemed like a worthwhile investment, so we gave him the rest of the bottle.

On Blue Beach we pulled our raft out of hiding. As we approached the *Sea Horse* in the dark, we signaled the watch with our small map-reading flashlight. Jep threw our bow painter to Ronnie and we climbed aboard.

"Do we celebrate?" all hands chorused.

"We sure do," I responded. Jep and I placed our remaining bottles on the table—what a pretty sight for our crew.

Out came our best mugs. We toasted VE Day and a quick end to the war in the Pacific. We all had another drink, but, oddly, few of us wanted a third. Again, we toasted those who gave their lives for this huge victory achieved against high odds. Then I said, "Here's to Danny, now he can go home to the Netherlands, from wherever he might be, and live in peace." Everyone fell silent, and we quietly hit the sack.

The next morning the crew talked about the whiskey we had consumed the night before. Everyone agreed that two drinks had been enough. The tropics seem to make alcohol more potent and when you don't drink regularly you lose the ability to consume much. Even the low-alcohol beer issued to us every few weeks satisfied our needs.

Getting beer cold took a little time. At our bases we got to know hospital workers and pilots. Baker had useful contacts and could often get hospital ice, a rare thing in the islands.

Our connections with pilots and ground crews provided tips whenever a repaired plane was due to fly slow time at high altitudes.

We would take our beer, a couple of cases of cans, to the airstrip and a crew chief would put it in a rear seat compartment. The pilot would fly at altitudes from twenty thousand to thirty thousand feet, where it was frigid. When he landed, our beer was chilled precisely right.

You had to have someone you could trust to deliver the warm beer and pick up the chilled cans when the plane landed. Otherwise it would be long gone.

The least desirable way to cool beer was to bury it in beach sand and pour 110-plus octane gasoline over it. When the gas evaporated, it cooled the beer. The problem with this method was the difficulty in getting the gas smell off the cans. Maybe that's why many Aussie pilots preferred their brews warm.

There was no room in our tiny refrigerator for the beer—and, besides, Cookie, the galley boss, wouldn't permit it.

23

Polka Dots and Pagadian

A FEW DAYS AFTER VE DAY, WE RECEIVED AN INVITATION TO ANOTHER wedding, which would take place in a week. The bride and groom were Moros, who seemed friendly to us. For our part we had given them soap and clearly weren't threatening. Jep planned to prepare a package of our trading material as a gift for the young couple.

After patrols we went over to the bathing pool. I don't want to imply that we didn't bathe before Malabang. We usually had to take saltwater baths with special saltwater soap, so we took advantage of every tropical shower or storm to soak in freshwater. The pool was sheer luxury.

One evening when we returned aboard the *Sea Horse*, Baker was with a couple of young Moro lads who had come to him for medicine. They had beriberi from lack of a proper diet and Vitamin C, which caused them to break out with small bumps on their skin. Baker decided to treat them with calamine lotion. He took a small cotton swab, dipped it in the calamine, and painted each of the bumps white. One lad was completely polka-dotted, and he was nearly finished with the other.

"Bake, what do you think the people will do when they see what you have done?" I asked.

"Skip, when I did a few dots on the first one, they liked it so much I did the other one."

Completely dotted, the boys climbed in their outrigger and paddled off to the village.

As we were sitting down to mess, one of Ron's favorite baked fish dinners, there was a clamor alongside. Men and boys from the village in outrigger canoes wanted to come aboard. Barzow warned them off but it was clear that they had something serious in mind.

I went up to the starboard rail and asked what they wanted. Pointing to one of the polka-dot boys, they gestured that they wished to have the treatment, too, even though they didn't have any bumps. The white dots were a considerable hit in the village. Baker gave them a bottle of calamine lotion and a swab.

Tower operations contacted us with a message that Colonel Jerome wanted to see me at headquarters the next day.

It was "no rush, not official business," according to the tower.

Jep dropped me off on our way out to patrol and arranged to pick me up in an hour at Malabang dock. Not official? Walking up to command headquarters, I wondered whether the colonel found out who got into his liquor chest. *I'll just have to pay up*, I thought. Booze was worth a fortune out here, but it was only money.

Colonel Jerome greeted me without much military pomp, just a salute, and put me at ease. By his manner I knew why his squadron would fly to the end of the earth for him.

"Lieutenant, yesterday runners from a small town up the coast came to us with letters requesting aid and assistance for the Pagadian people," he began. "The request came from the provincial governor and the commander of the guerrillas, who, as you might know, helped us establish MAGSZAM here."

Well, so far, so good, not a word about the liquor.

"I'm asking you to deliver medical and food supplies with your boat to Pagadian, as much as we can get together, as soon as operations can arrange it."

I told the colonel I would request, through the 13th Fighter Command, that a PBY presently covering air-sea rescue duty at Zamboanga add Malabang to its daily patrol area without disrupting its primary mission.

The colonel said he would order all supply units to issue surplus items on his list, and other things we believed would aid them. The runners returned to Pagadian with a note that relief would arrive in three days.

I left the colonel's office heaving a silent sigh of relief that the missing liquor on VE Day hadn't created a serious stir with the colonel.

Jep had the *Sea Horse* waiting when I reached the dock. When I told him to head to our anchorage rather than out on our regular patrol his left eyebrow lifted. Reading his eyebrow language, I knew he knew something was up.

I gathered the crew, explained the colonel's request and the need to get the supplies on board and sail to Pagadian. George and Whitey stood by to pack the items as they arrived and for the remainder of that day we took on gas and water and cleaned lockers.

Early the next morning, deck crewmen went ashore to gather items for the trip. Greeting my old whiskey-drinking VE-Day sergeant friend at the motor pool, I used the colonel's letter to request a weapons carrier to transport the supplies down to the dock.

Baker made out well at the base hospital, procuring quinine and atabrine for malaria, sulfa drugs for infections, pain killers, morphine and codeine, bandages, surgical tape, salves and lotions, and dozens of other medical items.

At food supply Ronnie had goods stacked the height of a double-ended dory: flour, sugar, powdered milk, cereals, canned goods, pots and pans, cutlery, knives and forks, paper cups and plates, plastic covers, seasonings, five sixty-pound bags of ice, and many other items.

Barzow came up with something that looked out of place. The aerial reconnaissance laboratory and photo unit gave him four full rolls of black sateen cloth (dull on one side and shiny on the other) used to create darkrooms where the photographers could expose and print the aerial intelligence photos.

"Rueben, what do you think the Pagadian people will do with the black cloth?" I asked.

"Skipper, when you're down to nothing, you'll find a use for everything," he answered.

It stayed in the shipment.

Jep and I went around to the PX and ships' stores and picked up miscellaneous stuff: lemonade mix, old candies, paper, pencils, crayons, chalk, and used books. After delivering these items to George and Whitey on the boat, we went to the chapel. The priest, rabbi, and minister gave us Bibles, songbooks, prayer books, and Hebrew readings.

After the crew came back aboard, George said, "Skipper, we had better have fair sailing and calm seas, because we don't have much freeboard left." George was right. The *Sea Horse* was riding low in the water. Full gasoline and water tanks, and the supplies, had the waterline up to the portholes. Generally, in fair weather, the ports were left open, but now they would have to be closed. But we were loaded, and the people at Pagadian would be happy to receive the aid.

Pagadian, a small war-ravaged Filipino town on a sloping hill, was about forty-five miles west-northwest from Malabang. We planned to depart from Blue Beach so we would arrive there about noon. The weather was beautiful and the sea calm. With our cargo, I was glad the sea wasn't running.

Jep trained his binoculars on the shore as the P-399 rounded the point at Pagadian.

"Holy smokes!" he exclaimed. "Look at the dock and shoreline." Dead tree branches marked the channels leading to the town, which wound through coral reefs.

He handed me the glasses, and I couldn't believe my eyes. Hundreds and hundreds of people crowded every foot of the bayfront. A couple of outriggers waited at the entrance to the main channel to direct the *Sea Horse* through the reefs to the crowded dock.

All went well until we approached the end of the dock. Many young people jumped into the water and were hanging onto the sides of the boat. I shut down our engines, concerned they would catch a leg in a prop. Jep directed them to back away from the boat, and we threw a line to the dock.

There was a lot of cheering. One might have thought General MacArthur had just arrived. I told the crew to stay aboard until we could determine how to proceed with dispersing the goods we had aboard.

Guerrilla troops opened a path through the vast crowd for their commander, Colonel Jerome's friend, who was accompanied by the provincial governor of Zamboanga Peninsula, the head of the schools, their Jesuit priest Father Reyes, and Doctor Rios from the area infirmary.

Welcoming them aboard, Ronnie brewed tea, which he served in our inspection coffee cups.

En route to Pagadian I had compiled an inventory of our cargo, which I handed to the provincial governor for distribution to the church, school, infirmary, and local population. I didn't want to get in the middle of a debate about who would receive what.

The governor wisely gave each of the civic departments the materials related to their needs. Once that was decided, the guerrillas brought in two-wheel carts pulled by a *carabao* (water buffalo) on which they loaded the supplies. I had no idea what everyone thought of the four rolls of black cloth.

Surprisingly the carts and *carabao* paraded up the village's main street followed by the school band with children playing flutes, pipes, and drums; our crew; local officials; school children; and some of the local guerrillas who were seasoned jungle fighters. Then came Father Reyes and the nuns from the Pagadian church.

A young woman with scraggly hair, wearing a ragged, but clean, dress, weaved in and out of the small parade as it slowly made its way up the main street. She had a manic expression and carried a dried cornstalk. I was to learn more about her later.

When the parade reached Dr. Rios's home, guests left the procession and went into a luncheon. The menu was modest—fresh fruit and baked fish—but this was soon after the Japanese pillaged the town before leaving the area.

I sat next to Father Reyes who started a polite conversation asking in what part of the US I lived. I replied that my home was in New York State.

"That's interesting," he said. "What part of New York State?"

"Upper New York State in the Hudson Valley, about seventy-five miles north of New York City. The city is called Poughkeepsie."

In fact, I lived in Arlington a couple of miles east of Poughkeepsie and about ten thousand miles away from this little jungle town in the southern Philippines.

Then he turned to me and asked, "How were things at Smith Brothers Restaurant on the corner of Main and Market the last time you saw it?"

I was stunned, and my expression must have shown it.

"It isn't so strange that I would know about your hometown," he said. "I lived near there myself for a brief time when I was a brother at the Novitiate of St. Andrews, a seminary about four miles north of Poughkeepsie. From there, I went to Maryknoll, and then I was given Zamboanga as my parish."

We had a lively conversation about Poughkeepsie, which I hadn't seen for three years. It was sure a small world.

After lunch we walked to the church, which the Japanese had severely damaged, smashing doors, windows, chairs, and the altar. There seemed to be no end to the insane destructiveness, including hymnals and prayer books.

Crude benches served as seating for the day's events. There was a recital with readings from school children and poems written for the occasion. The teachers and children had prepared the program in two days, which honored the Americans sent to Pagadian to save the children of their region.

The recital continued until early evening. Baker returned to the *Sea Horse* for a supply of candy Lifesavers, which the crew passed out to the children. The program was an excellent treat for all of us.

As we were leaving I met Señora Sansone, head of the church school, and asked her about the young woman walking through the parade with the dried cornstalk. A cloud passed over her smiling face and she cried as she related the story of this girl who had the run of the town.

She moved in and out of homes anytime, day or night. Everyone fed her and kept her washed. Shortly before the Japs left, they went from house to house looking for loot. This young woman was home with her baby while her husband, a member of the guerrillas, was away. The frightened young woman, clutching her baby, tried to get out of the door but was stopped. One of the soldiers grabbed her baby and smashed its head against the wall.

That was the girl's last sane moment. Every day she would get a cornstalk and go to the church graveyard and lay it on the baby's grave. This horrible story and the nature of war sickened me.

We stayed at the dock that night, promising to return on our Independence Day—July 4, 1945—and sailed with the early tide, returning to Malabang.

The PBY patrol hadn't received any rescue calls in our absence. This lack of action was likely due to skilled pilots, well-trained veteran ground crews, and minimal enemy resistance over the island's interior, where most of the Marine strikes occurred. We were always happy when our planes made it safely back to base.

Checking in with operations, I reported that we were back on duty and asked that Colonel Jerome be informed that his friends in Pagadian appreciated the generous relief for their town. A few days later, he flew over us at about five hundred feet, did a barrel roll, and gave us a "Well done 399 . . . four-oh!" He must have had a report from Pagadian.

One day while we were still at Malabang, I decided to find out more about the Moros. I was completely uninformed about their background and settlement of this southern island in the Philippines, which consisted of approximately 7,100 islands, 700 populated by 75 ethnic groups.

Jep let me off at the dock, and I walked up to the chapel to see the Padre, who invited me to have lunch at the mess. He inquired about our Pagadian mission, since he had provided church materials, and wondered how the people were faring after the Japanese left.

As we ate he related how the conflict between the Muslim Moros and the Filipino Christians had begun in the 1600s. The Christians drove the Islamic worshipers from the occupied land on the northern islands, forcing the Moros south to the heavily wooded jungle and mountains on Mindanao.

A few years later the Christians attacked the Muslim city-states on Mindanao and the Sulu Archipelagos and established a Jesuit base at Zamboanga. That was the beginning of the holy war, which still existed and had crippled the republic for centuries.

My only previous knowledge of the Moros were stories about those who had run amok at Zamboanga. There, an aggrieved Moro would go to the docks, hopped up on drugs, and try to cut and kill (with a Barong machete) as many Christians as he could in a murderous frenzy before being killed himself. These slayings were supposed to guarantee that the Moro would go to Muslim heaven.

After a few such incidents, Filipino riflemen were stationed on the docks to protect the men unloading ships. According to the Padre, when the Japanese invaded they stopped the Moro murders by executing the offender's immediate family and denying work, food, or clothing to others. The Japanese also flooded the island with worthless invasion money (just like the kind Bake and Ron had).

The Padre added that, like in all religious and political groups, extremist elements go way beyond the bounds of protest by using violence. There were many peaceful Moros, but none would ever get along with Filipinos. When I told the Padre about our invitation to the islanders' wedding, he said we should go but warned that all Christians should always be careful. As a gift, he suggested taking the young couple some powdered milk for their first baby but never give Moros meat.

Returning to the *Sea Horse*, I shared what I had learned with the crew and said I would stand watch for anyone wishing to attend the wedding and celebration. Barzow stayed onboard with me. After a couple of hours, we heard the party take on a loud, noisy, and happy tone. Beach fires blazed near the village where there were music and dancing. It sure sounded as if they were having a wonderful time.

Our outboard motor's sound resonated out of the darkness as the tender approached the *Sea Horse* with Baker, Ronnie, and Jep. George and Whitey had stayed at the celebration. Jep promised to pick them up at 2300 hours.

Everyone agreed that the food was good, even though they didn't know what it was, and said there were no alcoholic drinks.

Baker said they were happy people and that the young bride and groom, who spoke English, were friendly to them. They were pleased with the wedding gifts from our "goodwill" locker.

The crew could have stayed at the wedding as far as sleep was concerned. The loud sounds of the celebration carried to the *Sea Horse* all through the night. Some of the Moros slept while others played music and danced. When the sleepers awoke, they took up the musical instruments and dancing while the others slept. The festivities continued for three days and three nights.

On the third day the wedding drums fell silent when the bride and groom, in the last symbolic part of the ceremony, each took a leafy tree branch, waded out from the beach into waist-high water, and planted them next to each other in the sandy bottom. Cheers erupted as they splashed back to shore. These islanders sure knew how to party.

Word reached the P-399 that Colonel Jerome had a plan to persuade isolated Japanese troops to come in and surrender. The Marine pilots had been dropping leaflets, telling them they would not be harmed and would be fed. Only a very few had responded. Then he got the idea of having a high-ranking Japanese officer who had been captured in Leyte parachute into their camp to tell them that they would not be killed or harmed if they surrendered.

The officer selected was a Japanese admiral. The Marines dropped new leaflets announcing that one of their officers would be flown in and would parachute into their camp. The drop was too far inland for us to see from the P-399.

According to the report we received, the admiral jumped (or was pushed) out of a plane and floated down in his parachute into Mindanao's forested area, near the Japanese headquarters. Everything went according to plan until the admiral floated within sixty feet of a safe landing and Japanese troops shot him dead in the air.

The colonel had to work on a new plan.

Our mission was clearly winding down. Air-sea rescue missions had tailed off with the limited number of flights over the Moro Gulf. Headquarters transferred the *Sea Horse* to Zamboanga while assigning a PBY to cover Marine flights out of Malabang.

24

Zamboanga

On the Fourth of July we returned to Pagadian on our way to Zamboanga, making good on our earlier promise to the town.

In advance of our departure I met with Colonel Jerome and informed him that the 13th Air Force would continue to cover his unit's flights with PBYs and that we would be on call for him should he require a surface vessel.

When I told him we were stopping at Pagadian, I requested the same supply orders (chits) that he had issued for Pagadian on our last trip there. The colonel said he believed this part of the Pacific war would be over soon, and directed his executive officer to prepare the order, with special releases for drugs and equipment from the hospital. Most of the equipment and supplies would never make it stateside, or to another base, he said. So the people whose lives had been most disrupted should receive the aid.

I thanked him for his cooperation and, with a smile, for his liquor on VE Day.

"Oh, yes, Lieutenant Colonel Lang (newly promoted) told me about your midnight requisition," he smiled. "It worked out okay, he replaced it. Have a good mission in Zamboanga."

With that, I saluted and left.

Over the next few days we serviced the *Sea Horse*, gathered supplies for Pagadian, and stored them aboard. The crew bid farewell to their friends on the island who had helped us fill our water tanks, and we headed across the Moro Gulf.

The sail to Pagadian was relaxing. As usual we were approaching our next mission at Zamboanga without the slightest idea of our duties or the conditions there, but it sure kept things interesting.

Jep picked up the Pagadian dock and the channel with his binoculars. As on our first visit there was a large crowd gathered on the pier. This time I had some knowledge of the coral reefs and channel. With Bake on the bow, we slowly made our way to the dock.

Once we tied up, the commander of the guerrillas came aboard. After a warm welcome, he said the provincial governor had asked him to transport the supplies to the village's public building for distribution. The guerrillas posted an armed guard on the *Sea Horse* so we all could attend a luncheon at the hospital.

Pagadian citizens lined the main street as we strolled toward the hospital. This time there was no parade. The young, bereaved mother stayed close to us, with her dry cornstalk, and followed us into the hospital mess room. The locals in attendance paid little notice as she moved about the hospital.

Greeting friends made on our previous trip was a delight. Father Reyes, Señor and Señora Sansone, the church school's principal Dr. Rios, and the guerrillas' commander were pleased we had brought more goods for them, particularly for the church and school. Before lunch we sat on the long, wide-roofed verandah while hearing about the benefits of our previous delivery for Pagadian.

We observed many pairs of short trousers made from the photographers' black darkroom cloth by a remarkably busy tailor. Barzow was right. I didn't think I would ever see black on boys in the tropics. Señor Sansone said the black pants were now the latest style for boys. Nothing went to waste.

After a pleasant lunch, we toured the small hospital. The community had made great strides in repairing and refurbishing it. Only minor damage was visible. The clinic ministered to everyone from twenty to thirty miles around. Although treatments were somewhat primitive, those with severe illnesses or requiring complicated surgeries went to Zamboanga.

That afternoon the provincial governor gave me a letter to deliver to my commander, asking for help in clearing out the fifteen thousand Japanese troops trapped north of Zamboanga. General Jens A. Doe's 41st Infantry Division had already contained the Japanese within a perimeter, so I had no idea whether the letter would elicit action but I promised to deliver it.

That evening they had planned a Fourth of July fiesta for us. The traditional Filipino food was delicious. The evening's entertainment was memorable. The village's young ladies performed ethnic dances and sang songs in their native Spanish.

George and I were a captive audience, assigned to VIP seats with the governor and his wife, Señor and Señora Sansone, Doctor and Mrs. Rios, and Father Reyes. The rest of the crew let their hair down and had an enjoyable time, even singing some of the popular stateside songs, such as "Don't Fence Me In," "Don't Sit Under the Apple Tree," "Paper Dolls," and "Take the A Train."

The Pagadianons didn't want them to stop.

After a lovely evening, we bid farewell to our Pagadian friends. It had been a Fourth of July to remember. At sunrise, we embarked for Zamboanga.

The sail down to Zamboanga from Pagadian covered a distance of about 140 nautical miles along a coastline with deep bays and jutting keys. Trees, small towns, and villages were nestled in the bays and peninsulas along the coast. There were beautiful beaches, some with black sand and some with white sand. We stayed away from small ports, knowing the Japanese still controlled the interior.

The *Sea Horse* pranced along at cruising speed, running before the breeze like a three-masted schooner. Even George, Whitey, and both watches stayed on deck as we passed small islands and moved closer to the mainland shore.

At about 1300 hours, Jep raised Sacol Island, which was about twenty miles east of Zamboanga. By 1400 hours, we patrolled the docks, searching for a spot to tie up. I didn't want to anchor in the channel because there was a considerable current running through Basilan Strait. Finally Barzow spotted an old fishing shed (last used by the Japanese) with a surprisingly good wharf.

The shed was about a quarter of a mile from the main docks. We tied up and, to my surprise, found it unoccupied but littered with trash and in need of a cleaning. Since we had no means to haul the rubbish away, Jep and Baker caught a ride into town to find someone to clean the place and haul the debris away. George hooked up our water transfer pump and we washed down the *Sea Horse* deck and the outside of the shed and wharf.

In an hour or so Jep and Bake were back with four young Filipinos and a large two-wheel cart. In a brief time the lads worked hard and had the place picked up, swept, and cleaned. I paid them, but the cost wasn't too high for the wartime Philippines and they liked American money.

The shed was a gift from heaven. We had no idea who owned the building or had taken it over after March 10, when General Doe's 41st Division invaded Zamboanga and recaptured it for US forces, chasing the Japanese inland on the Zamboanga Peninsula.

We decided to stay until forced to move. It gave us the first chance in some time to unload and clean our lockers, bilges, and lazaret, and to store our gear and boat supplies. It also allowed us to give the *Sea Horse* a good cleaning.

The crew had a place to hang their laundry and dry our lines. We didn't store our trading material or our Japanese funny money in the shed; it was too valuable. We transferred a couple of heavy locks from our lockers to the shed's door.

We didn't have evening mess until late, and all hands were ready for the sack after their workout. Earlier some of the crew thought about going into Zamboanga City to explore but gave up the idea. Being tied to the small dock was a real comfort—the first we'd had since Morotai.

The next morning Jep let me off at the main Zamboanga dock and I walked to the 13th Air Force command headquarters where I learned that our mission was to cover the 13th Bomber and Fighter Commands. Our orders called for patrolling the Basilan Strait and not allow anything more substantial than a mosquito to pass from the mainland to Basilan Island and from the island to Zamboanga. We would be locked into the Zamboanga tower and operations shortwave to cover all rescue calls.

A real surprise came when they informed me that adequate dock space had been set aside for us on one of the main docks. There went our shed, my money, and a place away from the mainstream dock traffic with people continually unloading supplies for the area.

Hitching a ride over to the tower, I introduced myself to the on-duty tower operator and discovered we weren't strangers. The *Sea Horse* had been in their operations at Munda, New Georgia, and we had worked together at Biak and Sansapor.

The dockmaster assigned our mooring, which was suitable for quick docking and undocking. Because the tides weren't high, we only had to check our lines and fenders about once an hour. I requested a jeep to use for picking up supplies and was told, "We'll notify you." We received the name and intercom number for gasoline deliveries to our berth. The dockmaster arranged for a ride back to our fishing shack, which we were sorry to give up.

When I got back I learned Jep had allowed some of the crew to go into Zamboanga to look around and give us an idea of the conditions.

During mess Ronnie, Baker, Barzow, and Chaney described a bustling, overcrowded military installation in the center of a city once famous as a vacation resort city. It was only seven degrees north of the equator and enjoyed a beautiful, even climate, never warmer than 85°F and only varying up to nine degrees. Each evening around 1700, there would be a brief rain shower, which we used to bathe, although we had to hurry so we could rinse off before the storm moved on.

Zamboanga was the rainy season home of Asian rulers, high government officials, and business lords. The crew said our forces had leveled most of the luxury apartments and hotels when they drove out the Japanese. A few were still usable and were now headquarters for Major General Jens Doe's 41st Infantry Division, the Navy, and other units.

Ronnie and Baker said their most considerable difficulty was adjusting to a busy city. There were bicycles, jeeps, two-wheel carts, rickshaws, pony carts, and Army vehicles of all types. And noise. We had lived in a relatively peaceful world, so they were not prepared for the sounds of a bustling city in the southern Philippines.

Baker, always hungry, convinced Ron to go to a Chinese restaurant for something different for lunch. Three sailors from an oil tanker were seated next to them and had started a friendly conversation. They learned that these sailors were mad because they had heard about a brothel run and inspected by Special Services and had decided to try it that morning. When they found the brothel, however, there was a long waiting line. Next to it was another lengthy line, where GIs were waiting for free Coca-Colas. They decided to get in the bordello line. Gradually they moved up, passing the time jawing with guys in both lines. Finally, they were nearly up to the building when they discovered that the GIs ahead of them were receiving two cold bottles of Coke. They weren't in the brothel line after all, but the one next to it. Ron said these guys were bitter.

The Filipino government for Mindanao was restructuring, and many Zamboanga citizens were moving to Tetuan, a nearby suburban community, due to war-damaged homes and buildings in the city.

The next day I delivered the provincial governor's letter to 13th Air Force headquarters and arranged for our communications through operations.

Our orders, aside from rescue, were to patrol Basilan Strait to prevent small boats from crossing between Zamboanga and Basilan Island. The 41st Infantry had cut off communications between them. I was informed that we were near the top of the list to procure a jeep and to be patient.

When I got back to the *Sea Horse*, everything was shipshape and Barzow was on watch. The rest of the crew was aft on our awning-covered poop deck. I sensed something was up.

Jep met me on deck.

"Skipper, can I talk to you?"

"Sure, is it serious?"

"No, but it's important."

A young Filipino lad, about fifteen or sixteen, had asked to talk to the captain of the P-399. Jep said I wasn't aboard and inquired what he wanted. The young man, whose name was Miguel, asked about a job aboard the boat. After meeting the boy the crew liked the idea. Jep and I went aft and the crew started to tell me—all at once—about how useful he could be.

Although I wasn't against the idea, there were several questions to be answered. Would the boy's parents permit him to join our crew? Would our squadron commander approve it? Would sailing agree with him? What was his school situation? Where would he bunk? What about pay? Who would be his supervisor? No one could work for seven bosses.

Jep said Miguel would be back the next morning, so we delayed our patrol in the Basilan Strait until after we met Miguel and decided whether to bring him aboard.

When the boy arrived the next morning, I was impressed by his demeanor, confidence, and knowledge of the area. And he had a note from his uncle, with whom he lived, granting permission to join us.

Miguel had passed his first year of high school and would go into his second year. Although he was willing to work for half the amount offered, he was worth more. So we agreed on his pay and arranged for some new clothes for him. His valuable skills were speaking English, Spanish, and local dialects (Tagalog and Cebuano). A bonus was his experience sailing an outrigger in the Basilan Straits.

Jep said the crew would contribute to Miguel's pay since he would assist everyone. Hearing that, I upped the amount to eighteen dollars American. The crew heartily agreed. Miguel was thrilled and headed home to tell his uncle, with a promise to start the following morning.

It took a couple of days for the lad to adjust to our routines and enhance our lives aboard the *Sea Horse*. He was especially helpful to

Ronnie in the galley, preparing food and carrying it down the companionway, through the engine room, and to our aft living area where we ate. He swabbed decks and coiled lines, but most of all, was always cheerful. Jep gave him Danny's old bunk and he was officially adopted.

Basilan Strait was an excellent place to patrol, despite the strong current that came down from the Sulu Sea into the Moro Gulf. Cruising along the north shoreline of Basilan Island, we observed several plantations through our binoculars. Tropical gardens, sugarcane fields, rubber plants, coconut groves, and fruit-bearing trees surrounded imposing homes.

Lamitan was the main town in the north-central section of Basilan Island. It had a small dock area used mostly by traders and fishermen. The island was about thirty-five miles long, with major towns on both ends—Tuburan on the eastern end and Maluso and Santa Isabella on the western end. It also had a significant peak in its center.

We followed the Zamboanga Peninsula's shoreline up as far as Dumagasa Point on the western coast and Manicahan on the eastern shore during our patrols. These were the southernmost lines to where the 41st Infantry Division had driven the Japanese from Zamboanga. The 41st still maintained a heavily armed defense perimeter north of Zamboanga City.

We didn't spot any Japanese activity despite ten thousand enemy troops reportedly being in that area.

Our only air-sea rescue call was to cover a B-25 Mitchell bomber with engine trouble trying to make it to Zamboanga on a flight from Morotai. Barzow picked up the tower's communication with the B-25 and called the pilot to notify him that we were on his flight line.

"Good to know you're there," he radioed back. "Will keep you informed."

Fortunately he landed at Zamboanga airfield without getting wet feet.

As we tied up that afternoon after our patrol, an elderly Filipino was seated on the dock. After shutting down the engines, I went below. Soon after, Jep came to my quarters and said a Filipino man wanted to speak to me. On deck, I saw it was the older gentleman who had been there when we docked. He appeared to be a businessman, dressed in Army-issue chino pants, a stitched-front shirt, open sandals, and a handwoven straw hat that had seen better days.

"*Mabuhay*," I said, using a Filipino greeting. "Did you want to speak to me?"

"Yes, Lieutenant, I need to speak with you."

I invited him aboard. Seated on the deck over the sickbay, he explained his visit. After visiting family at Zamboanga, he hadn't been allowed to return to his home on Basilan Island. US forces had stopped all inter-island traffic by small boats across the sixteen-mile strait.

Anxious to return home, he had obtained a clearance pass from the military, but there were no vessels that could take him, except a patrol boat.

After conversing with him, I decided we could take him over to Lamitan on Basilan, assuming his clearance pass, which he dug out of his pocket, was valid. It seemed to be in order, stating that Señor Balias was free to return to Basilan Island. Barzow called operations on our short wave to verify the pass was authentic.

Operations said they would check and call us. Within half an hour, we got the return call with permission to take Señor Balias to Lamitan dock on our way to patrol. The old man's face lit up like the sun rising on a tropical morning and said he had a few personal items he would like to take with him. Thinking there would be no harm, I told him to be ready to come aboard at 0600 hours.

The next morning, as I was having coffee, Jep called me topside to take a look. A pile of boxes and bags, four fighting cocks in cages, and I'm not sure what else stood on the dock. Miguel had refused to help him load it on deck until I permitted him. I looked at Jep, and he looked at me.

"What the hell," I said. "We're in this deep and might as well finish the job."

Señor Balias and three young Filipinos brought it on board, with a lot of noise and confusion, along with the cackle of four fighting cocks trying to get out of their cages.

Finally we got underway. Señor Balias sat on his cargo to keep it from going overboard. Fortunately it was a short trip and we soon approached the Lamitan dock. A hundred or more people, who appeared to have a keen respect for the man, had been waiting for some time to greet him. Several came aboard, unloaded his belongings, and cleaned the deck. We didn't have to touch it.

Señor Balias warmly thanked us and asked for our crew's names, so I gave him a copy of our roster. As we backed away from the Lamitan dock citizens waved enthusiastically. It seemed a little strange that they would make such an event out of this old gentleman returning to the remote island. We answered their waves and headed off on patrol.

Operations requested we check a Moro settlement on the east shore of Sacol Island, which lay about eight miles east of Zamboanga. They wanted to determine whether there was Japanese activity on or around the small island. Since the Moros hated the Japanese and merely distrusted and disliked Americans, we hoped they would cooperate with us.

On visits to Moro-controlled districts and islands, we all wore side arms as a precaution against any hostile action. I brought the *Sea Horse* close to shore near the village and waited for them to come to the beach and invite us ashore, standard practice on our first visit to an island where we weren't sure how we would be received.

It was shallow near the beach, so we used our raft and motor to go ashore. As was usual on these visits, we took food to the villagers, which always pleased the women, particularly powdered milk and flour (usually cornmeal). We waited for the Emu, spiritual head of the village, and his followers. Miguel greeted them in their language. This pleased them, but they also spoke some English, making it easier to explain why we had come to their island.

Miguel and I walked up the path to the village while the crew stayed behind to watch the boat. The islanders seemed friendly and gathered around us. The Emu revealed that there had been no Japanese activity since March when Zamboanga changed to American control. Two

Japanese observation posts, initially set up to report on flights in and out of the Zamboanga airbase, were abandoned.

Our visit was going well when a potentially messy situation popped up. As Baker, Chaney, and Barzow were unloading our gifts, I decided to give the Emu a pipe and American tobacco, so I walked down to the tender. Ronnie had unloaded four cans of Spam. Offering pork to a Muslim is a major insult. If the Spam had gotten by me, it could have set off violent actions.

Grabbing the tins I quickly covered them with life preservers and told Ronnie to make sure the Spam remained hidden. Neither the Emu nor the islanders picked up on the potential *faux pas* and were pleased with the gifts. They invited us to stop whenever our patrols brought us near. I was happy to get the *Sea Horse* away from Sacol Island.

While on patrol we docked at Santa Isabella on the western end of Basilan Island, where there was a small field hospital. I wanted to talk to "receiving" for directions for bringing in rescued personnel should the need arise. That was often quicker than taking them to Zamboanga.

Walking through the small ward, I met a lucky, wounded young sailor. Japanese snipers were a constant threat, so the Navy base in Santa Isabella sent a squad of sailors to hunt them down. This young gob had been at the head of the group as it walked through the jungle undergrowth.

Snipers were almost always hidden up in the coconut palms, so the sailor was looking up. But a Japanese had dug and camouflaged a hole along the path. He fired his .25-caliber rifle and hit the young sailor directly between the eyes. Thankfully the bullet only creased the skin for about two inches.

I couldn't believe I was talking to someone who had been shot between the eyes.

25

Señor Atalano and the Underground Press

As we returned to our berth, a Filipino was waiting for us on the dock. He appeared to be a member of the Filipino upper social class, with an embossed shirt starched and ironed to a crisp. His demeanor exuded authority. I invited him aboard and we went to our rear poop deck where I asked about the purpose of his visit.

His name was José Atalano, the son-in-law of the elderly Filipino we had befriended by taking him to Basilan Island. He was very appreciative of what we had done and invited us to dinner at his home in the suburb of Tetuan, half of the crew one evening and the other half the following night.

Thanking him for his generosity in return for something that had taken little effort, we accepted the invitation and set the dates. Just before he left, he turned and asked, "Lieutenant, are you satisfied with your dock space here?"

"Yes, it's worked out fine for us."

"Have your requests for fuel and supplies been filled?"

"Yes, except for transportation, which we need to get the supplies to our boat. We've been promised a jeep and are on a list." Señor Atalano said he would look into it, and added he was looking forward to dinner and would pick us up the following Tuesday at 1830 hours.

The crew knew what had transpired already. Ronnie absorbed a few jabs about getting some real food for a change and threatened to not make the morning coffee. Everyone looked forward to a home-cooked meal.

As we were preparing to cast off for our next patrol, a young sergeant from the motor pool came aboard and asked me to sign for our jeep, which he was delivering.

"Who do you know, Lieutenant?" he asked. "Getting the jeep was no big thing, but they assigned you a preferred parking space near the dock. I thought only the big brass rated."

The sergeant showed me where our jeep and parking space were and gave me two keys, one for the ignition and one for the padlock on the chain around the steering wheel. The heavy hand of Señor Atalano was evident in this happy event.

The crew, including Miguel, drew lots to determine who would go to dinner the first night while the others stood watch.

Our evenings with the Atalano family were most welcome diversions and enjoyable. The Atalanos had two teenage daughters who entertained the crew by singing popular Filipino music and some stateside songs. Their home was a picture of tropical living, with wide-open windows, reed-woven roll-up curtains, floor matting, and sandalwood and teak furniture. The dinners were delicious. Even during wartime, the Atalanos seemed affluent, with a cook and maid.

After dinner the first evening, José and I stepped out on the verandah for cigars and brandy. On behalf of his father-in-law, he invited the *Sea Horse* crew to be guests of honor for a special occasion on Lamitan.

José said Papa Balias was planning a day-long celebration commemorating the Japanese ouster from Basilan, a thirty-five-mile-long island dotted with towns and villages. Papa owned and operated rubber tree plantations, with manufacturing facilities for processing raw rubber sap into bulk rubber, ready for shipping. He also owned sugarcane fields and a rum distillery, and raised cattle and water buffalo, or *carabao*.

The older man also oversaw the operation of the towns and villages, assisting them in fixing roads, bridges, water supply lines, medical clinics, churches, and schools. I was dumbfounded thinking about the old Filipino, who sat on the P-399 with his fighting cocks, being this Papa Balias.

The islands were full of surprises. I tried not to show disbelief to José, but I'm sure he knew.

José was the attorney general for Zamboanga Province and spent much time in Manila. When I told him that we would accept Papa Balias's invitation to the celebration but would have to clear it with operations, he said he thought they would approve it—another Atalano assist.

It wasn't a surprise when my commander, also invited, approved my request and traveled to Basilan with us. He stayed onshore Saturday night while we slept aboard the *Sea Horse*. With minimal air traffic in or out of Zamboanga, our PBY covered for us.

Papa Balias, or perhaps José, arranged for trusted guards to watch the *Sea Horse* when we weren't aboard. Miguel checked with the guards hourly and reported to Jep, giving the crew a break.

With the inter-island travel ban lifted, guests invited to the celebration from Zamboanga traveled to Lamitan aboard one of Papa Balias's supply boats. José and Señora Atalano, and their daughters, came with us aboard the *Sea Horse*.

Papa Balias welcomed everyone, including guests from as far away as Manila, saying this was an early celebration of the victory over the Japanese, which was a bit premature at the end of July. But after listening to the official reports of the collapse of the Imperial Japanese Navy and the Imperial Japanese Air Force (except kamikazes), it seemed possible that the end was near. Afternoon festivities and a feast highlighted the day, with musical performances and traditional dances.

We were in Lamitan for their early mass, and I was made *compadre* (godfather) to six recently born babies. Before the church service, I went to the Padre.

"Father, I see two big complications by my accepting this honor. I'm not Catholic and I'm sure the church would want me to be Catholic."

"Do you believe in God?" he asked.

"Yes, Father."

"Earl, do you believe in Jesus, the Son of God? Do you believe in the teachings in the Bible?"

"Yes, Father."

The kindly and reverent priest looked at me, smiled, and said, "Son, you have just been made a Catholic in the field."

I explained that the godfather of a child in America is responsible for backing up the natural father, which doesn't always work out. On the child's birthday and other dedicated events, the *compadre* gives a gift and spends time with them, usually lasting until the child grows into his teen years.

"I won't be on Basilan Island to help look after these children. I don't feel that it's proper for me . . ."

Interrupting, the Padre continued, "Son, Papa Balias knows the problem and will look after these youngsters as they grow on your behalf. He wants you to be their *compadre* and for these children to know that you, the captain of the *Sea Horse*, are their *compadre*."

So I relented.

The Mass, performed in Spanish, was a memorable, heart-warming event. I shall never forget the beaming, smiling faces of the young parents. Over the years, I have wished that I could go back to Basilan Island and find the now-grown children and tell them about that day.

José introduced me to many of his friends at the holiday luncheon, including a father and two grown daughters, named Robinson, who had migrated to the Philippines from Europe and had resided on Basilan Island for several years before the Japanese invasion. They lived on a plantation, running sugar and rubber refineries and a successful rum distillery.

Their land was about a mile and a half up the river from Lamitan. They invited the *Sea Horse* crew to visit the plantation. José urged us to accept the invitation to learn firsthand the hard-to-believe heroic story of how the Robinsons composed, printed, and distributed an underground guerrilla newspaper under the noses of the Japanese.

José said that despite constant surveillance, searching, and inspections of their home and mills by the Japanese, their printing press was never discovered. As we prepared to leave after the festival, we arranged to visit the plantation before returning to Zamboanga.

It's difficult to describe the island celebration adequately. One simply can't convey the happiness shown by these beautiful people or describe the mouth-watering aroma that floated from several open-fire spits, slowly turning quarters of grass-grown, baby beef steers and crispy roasted pigs. There were grills of swordfish, amberjack, sailfish, pompano, plus assorted shellfish, which were gently seasoned and cooked by Malaysian chefs. And what fruit—mangos, papaya, citrus, and several varieties of melons.

There were vegetables I had never seen or tasted before and desserts made from coconuts and Papa Balias's ice cream maker. There was also a variety of drinks served—teas, rice, coconut milk wine, a Filipino beer from St. Miguel brewery in Manila, and local light and dark rums.

The fiesta lasted for two days, with the festive sounds of music, singing, and laughter truly celebrating liberation. We sat with Papa Balias and José and marveled at the Filipinos, their stamina, and their enjoyment of the bounty of the islands.

The time came to depart, and to my surprise, Papa Balias embraced me. He was about five-foot-five, and I am six-foot-four. It was a gesture of true friendship, as we probably wouldn't meet again.

During our time on Basilan, Miguel would find me, once while I was riding a *carabao*, to report on the *Sea Horse*, assuring all was well. At meals I reconnected with the crew, who were enjoying themselves. Before returning to the boat, I mentioned we were going to visit the plantation and the clandestine printing operation up the river in the morning before returning to Zamboanga.

As Miguel was leaving he drew in a deep breath, and said, "Skipper, we have a small monkey on board since yesterday. I don't know how he got there, but he likes it so much that he doesn't want to get off."

A monkey!

All we needed was a little creature to look after. I could see the crew's gentle hands behind this acquisition so I couldn't blame Miguel. I'd have to settle this with my conniving crew.

Bidding goodbye to my new friends, I returned to the *Sea Horse*. The Atalano family stayed on Basilan with Papa Balias, but José planned to accompany us to the sugar plantation.

The hands were on board when I returned to the boat. I gathered them together and said I was aware of the monkey and would correct the matter the next day. They all feigned surprise (such fakers). I briefed them on the trip we were taking in the morning and said we were returning to Zamboanga after visiting the plantation.

Jep set the watches and we turned in.

The next morning, before José came to take us up the river, the crew introduced me to their pet monkey. It was tiny, not much larger than a small puppy, with a permanent smile on his face. It bothered me because it was early morning, and I had just had two days of overeating and late nights and there was no place on a working boat for this little creature.

I knew I had a problem when they called the monkey by name—Pepé—and recited all the reasons to keep him: amusement, raising the crew's morale . . . and besides, it wouldn't eat much. They'd all take care of him and he didn't make much noise. I decided to reserve my decision.

José had two dugout river canoes, each carrying three passengers and two paddlers, take us up the Lamitan River to the sugarcane plantation. Meanwhile, George, Whitey, and Miguel (and Pepé) stayed aboard the boat.

Before we left, José explained that an alarm system was in place to alert the plantation of anyone, especially the Japanese, traveling up the river by canoe as we were doing. Perhaps we were in the same dugouts, with the same paddlers, as the Japanese.

There was also a long, twisting, soft marshy road, with old bridges, that we could have used, but José said it was quicker and safer to use the river.

The ride upstream was beautiful, with its densely wooded shores filled with green, big-leaf plants, many with bright flowers and colorful birds. It didn't take long to reach the plantation's landing—a flat area near the river.

The compound sat on top of a considerable rise in grade, quite a bit higher than the river level to prevent flooding. The buildings were mostly standard Filipino commercial structures, with several imported metal industrial units featuring sliding doors and wide working and storage spaces.

The place had a unique aroma, due to sugar processing, the rum distillery, and the acrid rubber cooking vats. Our host's home was large and rambling, with a long, wide verandah built from reeds, palm fronds, and matting.

Mr. Robinson was expecting us—the alarm had worked—and came to meet us with his two attractive daughters. They welcomed us and served tea with coconut cookies on the verandah as we listened to the story of their perilous fight against the Japanese.

The Robinson family, including his deceased wife, had migrated to the Philippines from Switzerland when he was assigned to oversee his company's importing business in Manila. In the 1930s, after a few years in the Philippines, the company ordered him to return to Europe. His wife and daughters, who attended a girls college in Dumaguete, on Oriental Negros, wanted to stay in the islands.

Giving in, he sought investment to start his own import-export company. One of his business contacts was Papa Balias, who sold him one of his processing sites, complete with home, quarters for help, gardens, processing plants, and buildings and equipment. Along with the real estate came acres of rubber trees and sugarcane fields. Papa Balias also financed the acquisition.

Mr. Robinson said his businesses were going wonderfully well, and with his daughters' assistance he had built a significant export operation, which included shipments to Europe. He repaid Papa Balias's kindness by exporting and importing for him.

Disaster struck when the Japanese invaded the Philippines, quickly covering every strategic island with troops. They were oppressive. The only way he could save his home and export business was by turning over

60 percent of his finished products, fruit, and vegetables to the Japanese Zamboanga garrison. I assumed Papa Balias had to do the same thing.

The opportunity to strike back against the Japanese came when he met a major of the Philippine guerrillas from Zamboanga Province at Papa Balias's home. The major said there was a need to disseminate positive news to the people about the guerrilla war against the invaders, American victories in the South Pacific, and Allied successes in Europe against Nazi Germany.

Underground news would raise the hopes of the Philippine people, who only received propaganda from Japanese information offices and Tokyo Rose, who broadcast depressing and made-up stories. An underground paper would make General MacArthur's promise to return a rallying cry.

Agreeing, the Robinsons established the underground news operation on the plantation. In one of their sugarcane press buildings there were heavy Mindanao Mahogany cross-ceiling and roof timbers where they could secure a stable, chain-link, three-fold lift directly over the cane press. With the lift in place, it was easy to raise the press off the ground.

Trusted workers excavated a room with ceiling supports under the cane press area. They smoothed the walls, put in ventilation fans, and installed stairs, a desk, typewriter, and manual copy machine. The secret chamber served as the underground newspaper operations room supporting composition, printing, editorial, and shipping. An electric line buried in a hidden ditch running from the generator building to the secret office under the cane press provided electrical power. The alarm system with the Lamitan dock alerted the plantation about surprise Japanese patrols.

Obtaining fresh war news was a challenge with the Japanese jamming radio broadcasts. Paper and printing supplies were also in short supply. The guerrillas solved this by arranging weekly drops by an American submarine off a safe beach near Tuburan on Basilan. War news and printing materials delivered by the sub were transported to Lamitan by *carabao*, hidden under produce.

The chain hoist pulled the sugarcane press up and off its base, revealing the stairs going down to the printing room. The delivery of news and printing paper via submarine from Australia worked successfully, and soon the underground newspaper was being published about every two weeks in Zamboanga Province. From there it spread through Mindanao and adjacent islands.

Of course the Japanese learned the newspaper was being distributed and were furious that they couldn't uncover the source or location of the press. They checked Basilan Island and frequently inspected the sugarcane mills of our friend and his daughters.

With the alarm system in place, those upstream working on the paper had plenty of time to turn off fans and lights, climb the stairs, lower the cane press into place, and remove the chains and hoist and hide them before the Japanese arrived for a surprise inspection. Sweeping away tracks on the sand floor eliminated signs of the under-floor operation.

After much practice, they could come out, lower the press, and be washing dishes in the kitchen when the Japanese arrived. They searched every square foot of the buildings, particularly the house, and couldn't find the printing operation. After the searches, the Robinsons served rum to the Japanese, and sent a bottle to their commander.

These courageous people contributed much to defeat the Japanese in the Southern Philippines. As we prepared to return to the *Sea Horse*, I thanked the Swiss Family Robinson for their hospitality.

26

Rescue Appeal

THE DEEP ROAR OF THE TWO HALL-SCOTT ENGINES SHOOK THE AIR WHEN George hit the starter button at the Lamitan dock. This time it was accompanied by screeching and squealing as a dark, furry object sailed by my head, landed on the mast, and quickly scurried up to sit on our spotlight.

Pepé sat there chattering, and Ronnie couldn't convince him to come down. Finally he went to Miguel, who hurried him out of my sight—that thing had to go.

After docking at Zamboanga, I reported to operations to check whether headquarters had sent our next assignment. Zamboanga wasn't staging military airstrikes with the war moving north to the islands south of Japan, suspending regular air-sea rescue patrols. Our orders were to scout outlying islands for Japanese barge traffic between the Zamboanga mainland and the islands.

Jep suggested we cruise in the Jolo Islands near Borneo, south and west of Basilan Island. The crew was ready to sail in two days.

When you live aboard a boat, especially a small one, and are responsible for the safety of the people aboard, you're conscious of every little sound or motion with each change of wind and tide.

The next night, after returning to Zamboanga from Basilan, I was sleeping when I sensed something was wrong and found myself up on deck, still half asleep. The *Sea Horse* was drifting about twenty feet from our dock in small ground swells, only secured by our two stern lines. The bowlines were untied and trailed off the pilings into the water.

I roused Jep and he had all hands on deck to haul the stern back into the dock, secure the bowlines, and rig spring lines. Earlier I told him springs weren't necessary due to the small tide change. Once we snugged down the *Sea Horse*, I went back to my bunk. After consistently checking lines and then doing it again, I questioned how they could have come loose.

While we were refueling the next morning, I called the crew together and pressed home how serious it was to have the boat drifting free in the channel. Jep said he had checked all the lines the previous evening and they had been secure. I looked around. No one had an answer.

One difference about the evening before was that we had that monkey onboard. No one believed Pepé had loosened the lines, convinced he was too small and was in his box near the crew's quarters. But they agreed to take turns assisting the night watch to see if he went near the deck cleat.

I told Miguel we were planning to patrol the Jolo Island Group, which would allow him to visit his uncle in Zamboanga for a couple of days. Crestfallen, he begged me to let him go, saying he would visit his uncle as soon as we returned to Zamboanga. He also argued that he could assist us by speaking to the Malaysian people on Jolo, in their language. So, with the crew's urging, I consented.

The next morning it was 1100 before I realized that Pepé wasn't bouncing around the deck. Jep called Bake, who said sheepishly, "Skipper, I should have told you earlier. Last night, we caught Pepé up by the bow cleat. He hadn't untied the line but might have been trying. I sold him this morning."

Sold him! My problem was solved.

Jolo is a volcanic island in the Sulu Archipelago, about an eighty-mile sail from Zamboanga. The islands were about as beautiful a group as we had seen. Just south of Jolo was Tawi-Tawi, about forty miles east of wild Borneo. As we approached the island, dozens of small outriggers dotted the bays and lagoons. Jolo was the pearl center of the Pacific.

A typical scene would be a wife or son in a boat while the husband or father, wearing an apron, would hang on the side of the craft; take a deep, deep breath; swim straight to the bottom; pick up pearl oysters; and place them in his net apron. Surfacing, he would set the oysters on the prow and open them to see if they held a pearl—maybe even a rare black pearl.

The time the divers spent underwater was incredible, up to four and a half minutes. Dealers, primarily Chinese, purchased the pearls.

We anchored for the night at Tapul—a beautiful, romantic island. The crew wanted to sail to Bali, farther south of Tawi-Tawi, but the distance was too far for our allotted time. Local reports indicated there were no Japanese in Bali at that time. The next morning we headed for Zamboanga, by way of Santa Isabella on Basilan to pick up clear, fresh drinking water.

Later that day, when we docked in Zamboanga, a messenger delivered a note from José saying he needed to speak with me and would pick me up at 1800 hours. Even though he didn't ask me to bring anyone, Jep came along.

José was pleased to see us, and Señora Atalano, who had prepared a delicious island dinner, greeted us warmly. José poured us each a wee dram of Basilan rum and we went out to the wide verandah. For the first time since we had known him, he wasn't his usual smooth and self-assured self. As we sipped our drinks, José told us a family story.

Papa Balias had two daughters. José, a rising young lawyer, caught his eye, and he moved him into Filipino politics. During this time, José and Papa Balias's youngest daughter fell in love and were married.

A young physician who had interned in Australia and received his medical degree in Sydney set up his practice in Manila. The Zamboanga area in the late 1930s had antiquated medical facilities. Someone persuaded the young doctor to come to Zamboanga, where he met Papa Balias's oldest daughter, and they married.

There were no medical facilities in central Mindanao. The government told the young doctor that if he organized medical and surgical units for a small hospital, they would build one, stock it, furnish it, and staff it. He agreed on the condition that they would provide trained backup doctors.

Authorities selected Margosatubig, a small town located on Dumanquilas Bay, an arm of the Moro Gulf on the Zamboanga Peninsula, for the hospital. The medical facility opened to great fanfare throughout the Philippines as an example for other outer islands.

Then came the Japanese invasion and occupation. All communications between Zamboanga and Margosatubig were severed. Papa Balias's family lost contact with their daughter and son-in-law after the last message sent by radio before the Japanese silenced it. They said they were all right, had had a baby girl, and would contact them when possible. Japanese security shut off all news from Margosatubig.

A later message smuggled out of the Japanese-controlled area brought shattering news. The doctor was dead. A fisherman had carried the letter through Japanese security by concealing it in his hollow mainsail boom. The Japanese boarded and searched his small proa but failed to find the hidden note.

According to José, the tear-stained letter said the Japanese had discovered the doctor treating a guerrilla late at night, then tortured and killed him.

José's sister-in-law wrote that they were living with a large family and that the Japanese had not molested them. The surprise was that she now had two children—a boy and a girl. She begged for rescue and said the fisherman would help with a plan to get her and the children out. She also had heard a rumor that the Japanese might leave and centralize their occupation troops in north-central Mindanao.

During this long discourse, I sensed that José would ask us to rescue his sister-in-law and her children. José looked at me as though waiting for a comment. I kept silent and wondered, *What has this got to do with us?*

When I didn't comment, he said he wanted to speak with us first. He planned to go to the provincial governor and ask him to arrange for a rescue gunboat to bring out his sister-in-law and her children.

"I wanted you to know the background of this situation if they chose your boat for this mission," Jose said. "What do you think?"

I responded that our primary mission was to rescue, and we would consider it if headquarters approved the operation. I added that I couldn't speak for the crew since this was a civilian and not a military matter. Margosatubig might still be occupied by the Japanese, and it would be a case of the crew volunteering.

Jep said he'd put it up to the crew to decide. José replied that he understood, but time was critical because the fisherman had to return to Margosatubig. If he were away too long, the Japanese would know and be suspicious. With a date and time, the woman and her children could be ready on short notice. The fisherman was willing to take this dangerous risk because the doctor had once saved his wife's life.

I told José we could have an answer the following morning.

On the way back to the *Sea Horse*, Jep said he supported a decision to go if I would. The next morning I briefed the crew and told them I hadn't yet agreed, adding that their participation would be voluntary.

Savard asked what the odds were of pulling it off without alerting the Japanese garrison. I told him I wasn't sure the Japanese were still there, and that they could have moved out as they had at Pagadian. We would have the element of surprise, and by working fast we could be in and out quickly. But we still had to assume they were there in full force.

The mission's success depended on getting into Margosatubig docks silently, or at least as quietly as possible, under enough power for minimal headway. The mother and children must be ready to get aboard as soon as we touched the dock. We would cover ourselves with our twin .50-caliber machine guns. All hands would carry .45 semi-automatics. The amount of moonlight at 0300 hours, over which we had no control, would be critical. Some light would help, but we would be sitting ducks if it were too bright.

I told them to consider the risk involved seriously. Jep was to have the crew's answer by the time command headquarters authorized the mission, which I believed would be affirmative. Miguel would be left ashore.

Jose arrived at about 1100 hours, with the young Filipino fisherman-messenger.

Earlier each member of the crew came to me individually and said, "Count me in, Skipper." Miguel announced he wanted to be "with his crew," but the risk was too considerable.

After José introduced the Filipino fisherman, we went back to the stern cockpit to finalize the plan. Three nights later, we would arrive at Margosatubig dock at approximately 0300 hours. The mother and children were to be concealed near the pier and were not to come out of hiding until we came ashore for them.

Once our meeting ended, the fisherman sailed to Margosatubig.

When José announced that he and his wife planned to come with us, I explained that I thought that was an unwarranted risk. Disappointed at my reaction, he showed me headquarters' authorization to use the *Sea Horse* for the mission. As a lawyer, he had anticipated my rejection of his request. The general's executive officer had added, "Permission is hereby granted for civilian relatives to be aboard on this trip to assist the rescued woman and her children."

What the hell was I to do? He had written orders. Our occupying military brass was so anxious to have good, friendly relations with the local government that they made concessions. I told him to be aboard, wearing dark clothing, at 2200 hours on the evening of the sail, but to bring no luggage. Food, if they wished, was acceptable.

Operations confirmed our mission, which José had cleared through each of my superior officers and headquarters. Our almanac showed that the moon phase was favorable for our purpose.

The next day we prepared for the ninety-mile trip, filling fuel tanks and cleaning and putting our armament in readiness. Our plan called for Ronnie and Barzow to man the twin .50-caliber guns while Jep, Baker, and I, wearing sidearms, would go ashore and bring the mother and children aboard the *Sea Horse*. The mission was to be executed as quietly as possible with no shots fired unless ordered.

At 2200 hours, the Atalanos came on board. Señora Atalano declined my invitation to rest in my quarters, saying she was too excited to be still and preferred being in the stern cockpit with her husband.

The *Sea Horse* was up on plane, running like the thoroughbred it was on a beautiful night with light winds and calm seas. Flying fish sailed on both sides of the hull as we ate up the miles at about half our full speed, or twenty-one knots.

Our first course brought us to a coordinate about a mile east of Seboto Point on Olutanga Island. If conditions held, we could get a rough bearing off the dark, looming island point. If we were not too far west, we would keep the same course for another five miles and then change about five degrees for approximately twenty minutes bringing us into Margosatubig Bay. At that point, we would turn east toward the town at significantly reduced speed.

Luckily we could see the outlines of the island's points and peaks in the tropical night. We navigated using two stars, the first for about an hour, and the second the rest of the way to Margosatubig. It wasn't like daytime navigation, but it was enough to check our course. Baker was our lookout on the bow.

Our Filipino fisherman planned to meet us as we approached the town's docks assuming the Japanese hadn't caught him.

Baker came to the side of the bridge and said quietly that our guide was up ahead about one hundred yards. I cut our port engine and throttled down the starboard engine to near idle. Scanning the dock and nearby palm and bamboo buildings, I could see a shadowy figure and hoped it was our Filipino friend. There were no lights.

Expecting a Japanese spotlight to flood the *Sea Horse* with a glaring white light, we were nervous and tensions were high. Ronnie and Barzow were ready in the twin .50-caliber turrets.

Slowly we edged forward. I spun the helm at these low speeds to ease into the dock. The idling engine barely gave us headway. Baker threw a line to the Filipino standing by a broken piling.

The silence was deafening as Jep climbed onto the old dock, tied our stern, and came back aboard to the cockpit. If anything went wrong onshore, he would start both engines, cut the lines, and get out of there. Bake and I would take our chances with the Japanese if we couldn't return to the *Sea Horse*.

Our Filipino friend, Baker, and I crept toward the thatched buildings, where we entered a dark, unscreened room. There were two women and several children. In a muffled voice I asked which ones were going to the boat. The Filipino waved his hand. *All of them.*

Time wouldn't allow me to argue about it. I just wanted to get them to the boat and beat it out of this place. The two women carried and pulled the children down to the *Sea Horse*. The Filipino fisherman said the women had some valuable possessions to bring aboard as I reached for the starter button. Two young boys came out of the shadows carrying several reed boxes and woven bags and dumped them on deck.

As the pile grew I realized these women were moving all of their possessions to Zamboanga. When the doctor's widow came aboard, loud wailing, crying, laughing, and moaning replaced the silence. If the Japanese hadn't heard us by now, they never would.

Jep released the lines from our cleats, leaving the other ends tied to the dock. Both engines started with a roar and the *Sea Horse* headed past the small island guarding the harbor. As I looked back, something seemed out of the ordinary. There were no lights, even from homes.

Increasing the rpms, I pushed the *Sea Horse* faster than good seamanship dictated and against sound judgment. I wanted to get out of there but slowed down to pick our way around the point and then headed for open water.

The half moonlight was brightening. With Jep's help I got a bearing off the north end of Olutanga Island. If we were not on course, I could make a correction. We headed south-southeast to Seboto Point, reversing our earlier course with an adjustment for the current.

At about 0500 hours, the sky was lightening in the east and, for the first time, I could see the unholy mess on the deck. These women had brought along everything they owned, including garden vegetables.

Another surprise were the additional passengers, the fisherman and his wife who came aboard just as we were leaving the dock.

Then the jolt came. The fisherman revealed that the Japanese garrison had pulled out of Margosatubig the day before. All of that silent security for nothing. We could have come up during the day if we had known. José said he was sorry, and that he didn't know they had left, either.

About 0800 hours we docked at our berth on Zamboanga. I asked José to engage someone to clean up the mess—it wasn't the crew's job. He went ashore and returned with a Filipino man and a boy helper with a two-wheel pony cart to carry the luggage to his home. The deck was finally cleared and hosed down.

José pulled up with his Filipino jeep and the Atalanos thanked us for retrieving her sister and children.

The likelihood of getting sleep at our busy dock was slim, so we moved to the old fishing shack where we moored on our first day in Zamboanga. Miguel came aboard and was happy to see that we were okay. No one had taken over the shack, so we tied up at the dock.

Miguel stood watch while all hands hit their bunks, catching up on sleep lost the previous night. After a refreshing rest we cranked up the *Sea Horse* and went back to our regular berth. I radioed operations to report our mission complete. They responded, "Roger, standby for pending orders."

Another change occurred affecting the *Sea Horse* family when Jep was transferred to the P-613, nicknamed the *Seven-Up*, as acting skipper when Lieutenant Clyde Lorton left the boat. Jep's application for promotion to warrant officer was in process. Assuming it went through, he would command another crash boat. In the meantime he flew to Morotai where the P-613 was stationed.

In July Jep earned another battle star when he volunteered to fly aboard a 2nd Emergency Rescue Squadron PBY Catalina on a mission to cover a pre-invasion bombing raid on Balikpapan, Borneo, by the 13th and 5th Air Forces. The "Flying Cat" covered the strike by B-24 Liberators on Japanese gun positions and oil stores for sixteen hours and picked up two aircrews from ditched aircraft.

27

Nearing the End

On August 6, 1945, it happened.

With our intercom radio piped through the deck speakers, we heard the words, "atomic bomb" and "Hiroshima" mixed in with static and crackling. We all rushed to the radio shack and hung on every word coming through from operations.

Barzow switched on our long-range liaison radio. Listening to the news from San Francisco on station KGO, we heard more about the strike on Japan by an American B-29 Superfortress bomber called the *Enola Gay*.

A news commentator read President Harry S. Truman's official statement about the momentous event: "Sixteen hours ago an American airplane dropped one bomb on Hiroshima, an important Japanese Army base. That bomb had more power than twenty thousand tons of TNT. It had more than two thousand times the blast power of the British 'Grand Slam' which is the largest bomb ever used in the history of warfare.

"The Japanese began the war from the air at Pearl Harbor. They have been repaid many fold. And the end is not yet."

It was hard to comprehend the destruction that must have fallen on Hiroshima.

We all believed that the end of the war might be getting nearer, but knew the Japanese would fight to the bitter end. These people were suicidal about defending their homeland, which may have come from their early history of warlords and samurai warriors.

We anticipated a new assignment soon, and I thought, for the first time, about the real prospect of going home. The crew's morale lifted.

The overseas formula for service points, which determined who went home first, was complicated, so we each had to assess our status. The end of the war might still be a way off, but the attack on Japan gave us hope. All we could do was wait and continue to do our job.

José came down to the *Sea Horse* early the next day and invited me to his home for lunch. Papa Balias wanted to thank us "for rescuing his daughter and grandchildren." I told José it wasn't necessary, but he said Papa would be upset if I didn't come. About noon, I went to the Atalano home.

Papa Balias expressed warm appreciation for our efforts at Margosatubig and overstated the amount of risk taken by the *Sea Horse* and our crew.

And then he dropped another surprise.

"Earl, I asked José to invite you here so I could thank you for your help and make a business offer for you to join us when the war is over, which is, I believe, not too far off."

Papa had many business interests in the South Visayan Islands, including rubber, sugar, and distillery operations. Among his most lucrative ventures were Singer Sewing Machine agencies. Almost every home in the Philippines had a Singer. Sales of machines, threads, needles, and parts produced significant profits.

Forming a partnership, he would supply all existing and new Singer branches, including a parts inventory, trained repairers, and delivery by inter-island boats. I would be an owner-director with my headquarters in Zamboanga.

Continuing, he said, "After operating this franchise for ten years, you will return to America with at least a half a million dollars, and I believe more. Earl, this is an offer I would make to a son if I had one, and I would consider you to be like one I never had."

Papa's offer was flattering, and with the war winding down, I wasn't sure what the future held for me in New York. After being away for three years, I had no idea whether I could get my old job back. Sailing to the coastal towns and islands in the Philippines for peaceful purposes certainly appealed, but I knew it wasn't a practical option for me.

"Señor Balias," I responded, "I have a family and commitments that make it impossible for me to return to these beautiful islands, but I'll think about it carefully and let you know if I change my mind."

Papa said the offer would remain open as we parted, perhaps for the last time.

When I got back to the P-399, I had a message from operations to report the next morning. Everyone thought we would change stations. I didn't say anything to the crew about Papa Balias's proposal.

On August 9, the second atomic bomb fell on Nagasaki, with destruction similar to Hiroshima. Armed Forces Radio kept repeating that citizens in both Japanese cities had been warned of the impending danger if they didn't evacuate. No such warning preceded the Japanese attack on Pearl Harbor.

The following day, the Japanese government accepted surrender terms, which allowed the emperor to remain the country's sovereign ruler. That evening some of the crew were at the outdoor movie when they noticed that search lights were crossed to form a "V" in the sky. About that time, every gun on the island let loose. The Malabang airstrip anti-aircraft 90-mms let go with rapid-fire, celebrating the occasion. The next day we heard that all bases in the Western Pacific and the Philippines fired their ack-ack guns. Sadly, several deaths occurred from falling shrapnel.

On August 14, President Truman announced that Japan would officially surrender, and plans were initiated for a formal ceremony on September 2 aboard the USS *Missouri* in Tokyo Bay.

The war was over.

A letter Jep had written to Joyce months earlier pretty much summed up each of our feelings: "Just closed my eyes for a while and tried to picture what it would be like to be home. I daydream every once in a while. I hope I don't have to dream much longer."

Our squadron headquarters cut orders for us to sail to Tacloban, Leyte, and "standby" but didn't state when to report, so we could set our course through the Visayan Islands and take our time. At the same time, Jep and the *Seven-Up* departed Morotai, bound for Subic Bay in the Philippines, towed behind an LST, an 1,100-mile passage.

With the war over, our old gang was breaking up.

I told Miguel how valuable he had been to all of us, but he was upset that we weren't taking him to Leyte, as things were extremely uncertain. We didn't know whether there would be another mission or how much longer we would remain aboard the *Sea Horse*.

Miguel said his uncle would allow him to go and help him get back to Zamboanga later. The crew joined in and said if Miguel accompanied us to Leyte, they would pay his airfare home to Zamboanga when the time came. So I gave in. The grin on Miguel's face was priceless.

Headquarters cleared our trip, and we readied the *Sea Horse* for the voyage north. The crew wanted to leave from Lamitan and say farewell to our friends. However, I didn't want to explain further to Papa Balias why I couldn't accept his generous offer, so we left from Zamboanga.

I often wondered in the post-war years what would have happened if I had decided to return to Zamboanga and accepted Papa Balias's offer. I'm glad I didn't. If I had, I wouldn't have had my two great sons, Mark and Scott, both more valuable to me than all of the Far East's treasures.

28

Final Sail

WE LEFT THE DOCK AT ZAMBOANGA IN THE EARLY MORNING FOR THE last time. The sunrise was a thing of tropical beauty, and the freshened offshore breeze was almost like being brushed by an angel's wing.

Baker said he didn't believe we were changing stations since it almost always stormed when we went to a new assignment. I agreed, but I told him it was early, and things could change. There were only a few big white fluffy tropical clouds in the deep blue sky.

The *Sea Horse* made poor time, bucking the strong current of the Basilan Strait, confirmed when we checked our speed and took bearings off Dumagasa Point. We did much better as we passed Sibuco and planned to hug the shoreline to Coronado Point and then set our course for Oriental Negros and dock at Dumaguete for the night. The whole voyage was 235 miles, with the last and longest leg stretching 125 miles.

The Pacific's blue sparkling waters, wind, and sea conditions were perfect. The *Sea Horse* climbed up on plane, skimming the foot-high waves and ate up the miles while the crew kept watches and Barzow relieved me at the wheel every two hours.

Baker and Ronnie asked permission to break out the wind-up phonograph. Big band records, the soundtrack to our months in the Pacific, lent a sense of cheer to a pleasant passage.

At about 1700 hours, we made landfall at Siaton Point, on the southern tip of Oriental Negros, and then worked our way up the eastern coast, passing Dauin and Bacong. We finally reached Dumaguete, where we were fortunate in securing a berth for the night at a small wharf.

George, Whitey, and Ronnie went into town but were back within an hour with glowing stories about the rum and cantinas. I gave the crew shore leave until 2200.

Even though the connivers insisted that I join them, I remained aboard, sensing something was afloat. All of a sudden, after all of these months, they wanted my company at a bar. Finally they gave up the idea and strolled up the road to the town's center.

The next morning the crew nursed hangovers from Filipino beer and white-lightning rum. One of them admitted that George and Whitey had planned to ply me with rum and set me up with a girl for a few pesos. The others wouldn't go along, so they dropped the idea.

At 0900 we hauled our lines and embarked for Tacloban, planning to arrive by evening. The crew's heads were a little smaller by then. Barzow and I alternated turns at the helm on another gorgeous sailing day, with our course set for Mactan Island, across the channel from Mandaue, Cebu.

Ferdinand Magellan, the Portuguese navigator and sailor, visited Mactan Island while in Spain's service in 1521. In his historic around-the-world exploration, he discovered these islands, five hundred miles southeast of mainland Asia. They were later named the Philippines in honor of Prince Philip, who became Philip II of Spain.

Spain retained possession of the Philippines for the next 350 years, ceding them to the US after the Treaty of Paris, signed following the Spanish-American War in 1899. There was a monument to Magellan on Mactan, where he was killed and buried after a battle.

Arriving at Mactan we tied up at one of several docks at Opan Shipbuilding & Slipway Corporation, with a small dry-dock and a marine railway with cradles. The proprietor, seventy-one-year-old "Dad" Cleland, came down to meet us, recognizing the *Sea Horse* as an air-sea rescue gunboat.

After introductions I explained that we were bound for Tacloban as our mission drew to an end. The boatyard had a full-service contract with the US military.

George and Whitey refueled the boat while the old salt invited me into his office, which I suspected held records for every small craft that plowed the waters in these beautiful islands.

As I described our work in the South Pacific, he was surprised that we had had only minor breakdowns. Replacing an engine, cracking our bronze rudder strut at Guadalcanal, and bending a propeller fin blade when we struck a submerged coconut log, were relatively insignificant, considering the miles the *Sea Horse* had covered. Our engines ran without their earlier smoothness, requiring more and more service, but both had performed well for an excessive number of hours.

Cleland briefed me on what loomed ahead for us, urging extra caution going through San Joaquin Strait, between Samar and Leyte. The narrow channel running between the Samar Sea and Leyte Gulf could be tricky, with a powerful and turbulent current, sandbars, and swirling undertows affecting our ability to hold a course.

It might have been wiser to go east through Surigao Strait, but we decided to go along the western coast of Leyte in the Comotes Sea, pass by north Cebu and Masbate in the Visayan Sea and through the San Joaquin Strait down to Tacloban.

The next morning, with perfect weather, we set sail for Biliran Island, where we would layover before tackling the San Joaquin Strait. We stopped briefly at the alluring Camotes Islands and wished we could have spent more time there.

At about 1130 hours, we put into Tabango, Leyte, looked around, and enjoyed fresh eggs and Philippine coffee. A leisurely sail to Biliran Island left us with plenty of time to sail on to Santa Rita, Samar, at the San Joaquin Strait entrance. We anchored there, and I worked on reading the tide. We missed the slack tide, the best time to tackle this strip of water, so I decided to catch it the next morning. No one asked for shore leave at Santa Rita. Thoughts were turning more and more to our homes.

After mess we discussed the points each of us thought we had to our credit, establishing our eligibility to return to the states for discharge. Although the crew bantered about returning to America, I sensed a note of sadness as they discussed our immediate future and the *Sea Horse's* fate after the war. *I'll face that when the time comes,* I thought to myself.

During the night I checked the tide a couple of times. The next morning we shoved off into San Joaquin Strait, our final sail to Tacloban, which was only about twenty miles south-southeast.

As we navigated down the channel, the *Sea Horse* bucked a current, passing several dangerous places with sandbars and obstructions. With our advanced knowledge of the conditions, we reached Tacloban without incident in an hour and a half.

Sailing down the docks we saw a gunboat flotilla, 63-, 85-, and 110-footers moored next to each other row on row in twos. As we backed into a dock beside Marv Pelser's P-400, at least twenty hands reached for our lines in greeting—what a great reunion. We hadn't seen each other in many months, some of us as far back as New Orleans. A lot of saltwater had passed under our hulls since then.

Orders awaited us. The *Sea Horse* was one of the boats to be turned over to the Philippine government. We were also to train a Filipino crew so that they could operate the P-399 for inter-island services. In the meantime, we were to clear out our gear. The ship's log was to remain with the *Sea Horse*. If I had known then what I know now, I would have packed that precious chronicle with my gear.

In the next few days at Tacloban, we conferred with local coastal control officials who would assume responsibility for the P-399 and its new Filipino crew. I couldn't help feeling like I was abandoning an old friend who had been so dependable and responsive in every situation we had experienced.

Our memories would be unforgettable, like gliding into a rising sun after a long night mission as it came up over a palm-fringed island, bathed in all the glorious colors of an early-morning sky. And there were times when conditions were just the opposite, with fifteen-foot waves crashing into the bow, spraying green water over the partially protected flying bridge. When the *Sea Horse* dove off the tops of these typhoon-driven seas, down into their troughs, we knew, without any doubt, that the *Sea Horse* would pull up out of it and sail to a safe harbor.

Whether called a cyclone, as in Australia, or a typhoon, as in the Far East, with the scuppers running frothy white and the only communication between crew members being shouts over the storm's roar, there was never a doubt that the P-399 would bring us through. She was dependable under enemy fire when her maneuverability allowed us to bring our twin .50-caliber machine guns to bear as we took evasive action.

On the *Sea Horse*, we didn't conquer the Pacific—no one will ever truly defeat the sea. We contributed sound seamanship and the P-399 did the rest. Consistent reliability caused us to consider the *Sea Horse* a moving part of our lives and our fortunate survival.

As I cleaned out my desk and quarters, I removed the varnished wood plaque in the wheelhouse that had "Donated by the Citizens of Augusta, Kansas" in raised letters. It had been an inspiration to the crew who patted it at times as we passed the bulkhead. I sold my sextant, purchased in San Francisco, for an inexplicable reason, and packed my trusty Navy-issue Colt .45 semi-automatic, which was later removed from my seabag by way of a long knife slash across the top.

As instructed, I burned papers and cleaned files, preparing to leave the *Sea Horse* when we received orders to sleep aboard and eat in the base mess hall.

Evenings aboard, we sat idly on deck with other skippers, all of us waiting to leave. I couldn't acclimate to the reality that I would be quitting these decks shortly after walking them night and day for nearly two years. Turning the *Sea Horse* over to the Philippines was hard. In the years to come, I wouldn't forget the sheer joy of her response to my controls or the exhilaration we experienced when this thoroughbred stepped up on plane, dancing on the sea.

With the Filipino crew aboard, we instructed them in the P-399's operations and had them set a course for Marabut, Samar. After repeating this navigational calculation three times, they still couldn't grasp it. These were fine young Filipino lads—two had gone to college—but they required extended instruction in boat handling and dead-reckoning navigation.

Another problem was that they wanted to run the P-399 at full speed and didn't understand that the boat didn't have automobile brakes. My hunch was that the *Sea Horse* would wind up on an island shore if they didn't change their approach. If I could have purchased and shipped it home, I would have done so. Instead we got it ready for the transfer.

It was time for Miguel to return to his home in Zamboanga. You would have thought the crew was parting with a son. While there were no visible tears, the sadness surrounding them was much like the day Danny went aboard the hospital ship *Comfort*.

Since the morning we met Miguel on the dock in Zamboanga, an extraordinary bond had developed with the crew. Miguel, of course, wanted to go to the US with us. We explained why that wasn't possible, but the boy couldn't understand.

I didn't go to the small Tacloban airport to see Miguel off, but that wasn't the last time I saw him. The crew left him to wait for his plane to Zamboanga. Once they were out of sight, Miguel hitched a ride back to the docks and was at the *Sea Horse* when they returned, so they had to take him back to the airstrip. This time they stayed with him until the plane departed.

Good lad, Miguel.

29

Destination America

DESTINATION AMERICA LOOMED LARGE FOR EACH OF US.

The big job now was to get the crew's names before headquarters, which had moved to Clark Field north of Manila in the Philippines, to obtain orders for each man qualified for transfer back to the States. George Savard was immediately eligible and the first to leave on a flight in a vacant seat on an Army DC-5 transport that was taking back hospital patients.

Each time someone left for home, it was like an open wound that would eventually mean the end.

Next came Ronnie and Baker, who flew to Clark Field in mid-September and connected with Jep. Once the war ended, Jep had withdrawn his application for promotion to warrant officer, anxious to return home to his growing family.

Luckily, Baker was assigned a seat on a flight back to the States.

Ron and Jep had berths aboard the Liberty ship *Juliette Low* and departed Manila on September 28, routed through the Panama Canal to New Orleans.

Their voyage to the States was a pleasure cruise compared to what Whitey, Reuben, and I experienced nearly two months later. The *Juliette Low*—named for the founder of the Girls Scouts of the USA—only made ten knots an hour and covered about 250 miles a day. Jep and Ron each shared a stateroom with another returning veteran and ate in a dining room served by stewards.

The ship still had an abundance of ammunition aboard for its 5- and 3-inch guns and 20-mm cannons. For entertainment the Navy gun crew allowed the fourteen passengers to fire the weapons until boredom set in. Then the remaining ammo was dumped overboard. Sunning on deck was also a popular pastime during the two-month trip.

After a week's layover in Panama, the *Juliette Low* embarked for New Orleans. As the ship approached New Orleans early one morning in late November, she made a sweeping turn and headed around Florida and up the East Coast bound for Baltimore. Ahead of reaching port, the fourteen veterans aboard learned they would have to clear US Customs.

Years later Jep recounted, "When the ship docked, there was a rush for the gangway and we never saw a Customs agent."

Ronnie and Jep headed across the street to a bar and ordered beers. "While we were sitting there looking in the mirror, we decided to get haircuts," said Jep. "So we went to a barbershop, then headed back to the bar. Looking in the mirror again, we decided that everyone at home knew us with short hair, so we went back and had another haircut."

Two days later, they were on a train bound for Chicago and a long-awaited reunion with their wives, Jep with Joyce, and Ron with Ruth.

These separations were emotional. We struggled not to let it show, knowing that this was probably the last time we would ever see each other after nearly two years together. The remaining *Sea Horse* crewmen were soon ordered to Clark Field, north of Manila, on Luzon, to stand by until our departure date.

The rows of silent crash boats tied up near the P-399 appeared lifeless. It was a sentimental moment, having a last look at these magnificent boats that had performed so well. Stepping off the *Sea Horse* for the last time, I was glad no one watched as I gripped the cable rail with my head bowed. After a bit, I lifted my seabag to my shoulder and made my way, without looking back, to a waiting six-by-six cargo truck that would take us to Tacloban airstrip and the plane to Clark Field.

When we landed at Clark Field near Angeles, we saw and heard our first jet aircraft—the future had arrived. At that point we split up because of rank. It took me a while the next day to locate Barzow and Whitey.

Still waiting for orders near the end of October, I took the opportunity to be a tourist, visiting places near Clark, like Baguio summer resort and Conception. This quiet period gave us a chance to reflect on the war years and ponder the events we participated in during our journey from the Fijis to Luzon.

Finally the word came—moving orders. We boarded a Philippine Railway troop train (cattle cars) and rode it to Manila and Cavite, where Barzow, Whitey, and I boarded a troop transport bound for the US, along with what seemed like five thousand other GIs. The ship sailed for the US as soon as it was loaded, which turned out to be a mistake.

A high-powered typhoon hit Luzon about the time we were leaving, and it was headed east-northeast, on the same course as the transport. Our voyage was long and miserable. The ship and typhoon traveled at the same speed and we sailed in its high wind and mountainous seas for fifteen days.

The breakers lifted our stern and props ran free out of the water, impeding the headway necessary to drive us out of the storm. The ship shook and shuttered. Most of the passengers were seasick, and when Barzow, Whitey, and I went to mess, we were among the few aboard who wanted to eat. Even with that, food ran out in ten days.

Eventually, the Golden Gate Bridge was a welcome sight. Barges and fireboats decorated with "Welcome Home" signs greeted the ship. We disembarked at Pier 15 and boarded ferryboats, which took us to Stockton to wait for transportation east and discharge.

Onshore once again, we were tired and hungry. Hunger won out, and we went to a mess that had everything we hadn't seen for nearly three years—milk, lettuce, steak, tasty rolls, salads, turkey, French fries, ice cream, pie, and superb coffee. The food didn't make up for the Spam, fish, and K-ration meals we had eaten, not counting those with Papa Balias and José Atalano and on Kiriwina Island. This was real, stateside food.

After gorging ourselves we collapsed on our unmade bunks. The next day a few officers and I went to Navy supply to get warm clothes. All I had were summer-weight chino pants and shirts. A seaman's peacoat came in handy because I couldn't handle the crisp December nights in Northern California.

I contacted Reuben and Whitey, agreed to meet in Oakland and stay over until our trains pulled out. The next day we checked into a hotel. Reuben and I were traveling east but had separate reservations. Whitey, whose home was in Southern California, decided to stay over with us.

Their trains were scheduled to leave the next afternoon, and mine the following day. That evening we each bought a bottle of liquor, Three Feathers in my case for old time's sake. And then we went to a fine restaurant. Afterward we went back to our rooms to drink, but we each had only one or two.

A glass of Three Feathers brought back memories of past celebrations. Rueben had champagne, and Whitey had scotch. The reason we didn't drink much was that we were busy taking showers. One after another of us jumped into one of the two room's showers to make up for all the saltwater baths we had endured. This fresh, gushing water made us feel as clean as we did at the waterfall on the island off Malabang, Mindanao.

Reuben's train east was leaving at 1430 hours, and Whitey had a seat booked for Los Angeles, so they asked me to ride over to the station with them in a cab. It was raining.

We got out of the cab across the street from the entrance to the terminal. To my great surprise, they saluted me and said, "So long, Skipper." Picking up their gear, they hurried through the rain to the terminal, never looking back.

I stood there, with the cabby looking at me, glad it was raining—an excuse for the water running down my face. The cab driver got out, loaded me and my memories into the taxi, and drove me back to an empty room.

Afterword

On a wintry afternoon in early 1995, sitting in my study in our hilltop home in rural eastern Iowa, I sat at my desk, pondering a poignant letter of condolence written to my mother by Earl McCandlish. Nearly four months had passed since my father's death. In that time, I had struggled with a deepening urge to fill in the lines in Dad's recollections from his time aboard the *Sea Horse* during World War II.

Always referred to as "Skipper" in our home over the years, Earl McCandlish was the only living connection with the P-399 as far as I knew. So, on an impulse, I found his number online and called. He picked up his phone in Poughkeepsie, New York.

Although in his early eighties, his strong voice immediately brought to mind the familiar black-and-white photo of a movie-star-handsome fellow with a Clark Gable mustache, wearing a crushed Army Air Corps cap, holding a terrier puppy named Salty. As a boy, that image, along with a dogeared picture album chronicling the *Sea Horse* and her crew, kept me occupied for hours.

In the late 1940s and 1950s, I would slip quietly into our cellar and open an old, hump-backed wooden trunk tucked away in a corner. Inside the musty-smelling chest were albums of black-and-white photos, official AAF reports on flimsies (carbon copies), a Silver Star in its navy-blue case and campaign medals in their original boxes, and a grass skirt smelling of the South Seas—all chronicling Dad's service as the first mate aboard the P-399.

Over the years Dad slowly shared his wartime memories, experiencing a full spectrum of emotions, from great humor to supreme sadness.

"One thing about our work, we saw the better side of the war," he wrote in a letter to his parents on September 12, 1945. "I am really glad that I was able to do this kind of work. It gives one great satisfaction to save a man's life rather than kill. Thank the Lord that I only have a couple black memories to forget."

Over the years his emotions only revealed one dark moment, the sudden loss of the P-38 pilot who crashed next to the P-399 off Guadalcanal. On another occasion he started to tell me about an incident on Morotai when he was in a tent field hospital suffering from malaria. One night the Japanese infiltrated the camp and hand-to-hand fighting ensued. At that point he stopped and changed the subject, so I'll never know what occurred, but I have my suspicions.

On November 24, 1989, he agreed to sit down for a recorded interview, during which he revealed more details about life aboard the *Sea Horse*. Soon after, he was diagnosed with pancreatic cancer and began the battle for his life, which miraculously lasted for almost another four years. During this time I tucked the audiotape away.

After his passing my mother turned to a shoebox full of bittersweet memories, Dad's letters to her from the Pacific. Now and then she shared stories with me, but I always felt there was much more to be known. One afternoon while I was visiting her, she pulled out a light-blue envelope and passed it to me. It was addressed to her, and on the reverse side was a return address for "E. McCandlish" in Poughkeepsie. Reading his eloquent words rekindled my desire to dig further into the *Sea Horse* story.

As I introduced myself during our initial phone call, I had no intention of writing a book. But as that first conversation progressed, I knew there would be more. Sure enough we chatted three or four times within a few days, and with each new story, the idea for a book evolved.

One evening I asked whether he had considered writing his memoirs. The stories were too bountiful not to document. Histories and memoirs from World War II written in the years following the conflict spill off bookshelves in libraries, but not a single volume had been recorded about the air-sea rescue boats dispatched to the Pacific. "I've been waiting fifty years for someone to ask," he declared. And so *Crash Boat* was launched.

Over the next few weeks he reached back to 1943 and wrote down on yellow legal pads his memories and then mailed them to me. As each packet arrived I transcribed them into a computer-based document. The process carried on for nearly five years, with frequent phone conversations in between. A complete picture of life aboard the *Sea Horse* took shape little by little, filling in what I already knew. For two summers my wife, Amy, and our daughter, Jane, who lived in Manhattan, traveled by rail from New York City to Poughkeepsie.

Stepping off the train the first time, I looked up the stairway to a pedestrian cross-bridge and immediately saw Skipper, with a shock of gray hair, a clean upper lip, and a broad smile on his face. Moving ahead of the girls I took the steps two at a time. Rounding the corner at the top, we both stood briefly staring at each other, and embraced. These visits closed the *Sea Horse* circle for me, a process that had begun soon after the war ended.

Sitting in Skipper's apartment we pored through his official records and souvenirs from the Pacific, including a Japanese flag, as he recalled the war years aboard the sleek wooden crash boat. At one point, he handed me a piece of white canvas with "*Sea Horse*" neatly lettered in black ink across it. The "S" was in the shape of a seahorse, with "P-399" picked out in white.

"Your dad made that for me while we were overseas," he said. "I'd like you to have it."

By mid-2000 we had a rough manuscript. To preserve Skipper's chronicle, we had it privately printed. In late October, I made several attempts to contact him by phone, leaving messages each time. One evening I received a telephone call from his son, Mark, with the sad news that Skipper had died during emergency surgery.

As far as I knew, that was the end of the story. Our dear friend was gone, but we had completed his memoir—or so I thought.

In late 2019 Tom McCarthy, an acquisitions editor for Lyons Press, read the original manuscript and offered to publish it. Over the last two decades, much more information and official records from the war had become available. After my mother died in 1999, I read Dad's letters, which contain a treasure trove of contemporary details supplementing Skipper's recollections.

As I went back over the manuscript and did additional research, I wondered what had happened to the other men who rode the *Sea Horse* from Guadalcanal to the Philippines. After the war the crew had returned to civilian life and never reunited as a group.

It turned out that Earl McCandlish was the last surviving member of the P-399 crew. Returning to the Poughkeepsie area in early 1946, he and his wife, Martha, raised two sons, Scott and Mark. During a city government career, Skipper served Poughkeepsie as Assessor, Planning Board representative, and Zoning Administrator. Later, he was a commercial real estate appraiser. On October 30, 2000, he died at age eighty-nine.

Dad returned to Marquette in Michigan's Upper Peninsula to his position as a draftsman with a chemical company. On weekends he and his father ran a deep-sea fishing charter on Lake Superior aboard the forty-two-foot yacht *Lady Isabel*. In 1951 he accepted a position with a pharmaceutical company in Lower Michigan, working for thirty-two years in engineering. Mom and Dad were married for fifty-one years. At that time, our family grew to six, with my sister, Norma, and brothers Bill and Tom. Dad died at age seventy-four on September 16, 1994.

George Savard continued to live in Honolulu, Hawaii, after the war with his wife, Thelma. He worked as manager of facilities and ground equipment for Hawaiian Airlines until his death on December 17, 1966, at age fifty-one.

Ronald C. Albrecht returned to Milwaukee, Wisconsin, where he and his wife, Ruth, raised a son, Ronald, Jr., and a daughter, Kim. Cookie died on August 19, 1998, at age seventy-seven.

Wilson G. Hollis went back to Bessemer City, North Carolina, after his discharge. Wilson and his wife, Virginia, raised their son, Gary, and owned and managed a local business. He died on December 27, 1996, at age seventy-five.

Homer L. Baker, Jr., returned to Cumberland, Maryland, where he and his wife, Mary, had two daughters, Margaret and Nancy. Retired from the City of Cumberland Street Department, Bake passed away on February 7, 1999, at age seventy-seven.

Reuben Barzow, who replaced Wilson Hollis as radio operator, moved from New York to Los Angeles in the 1950s, where he operated a family business. He and his wife, Adeline, had a son, Phillip. Reuben died on January 9, 1998, at age seventy-nine.

The last time any of the crew saw or heard from Danny Tholenaars was the night he was transferred to the hospital ship *Comfort* off Hollandia.

A great shock came when I discovered that William C. (Whitey) Chaney returned to Hermosa Beach near Los Angeles after leaving Skipper and Reuben in San Francisco. A day or two later, on December 17, 1945, he died from accidental carbon monoxide inhalation at age twenty-three, a tragic loss of this courageous young man. Whitey was survived by his wife, Mary.

During the research for *Crash Boat* I wanted to learn more about the Royal Australian Air Force pilot the *Sea Horse* crew attempted to rescue during the battle of Galela Bay. The answers resided in the National Archives of Australia.

James William Brighton Lennard had turned twenty on October 21, 1944, two months before his P-40 Kittyhawk fighter sustained hits from enemy antiaircraft fire and crash-landed on the Galela Bay beach.

His home was in Naracoorte, South Australia. He enlisted on March 27, 1943, and joined the 80 Squadron when it formed at Townsville, Queensland, in September 1943.

As Dad and Whitey swam toward him in Galela Bay, they saw he was face down in the surf. Skipper deemed it too dangerous to try and recover his body. It was believed that Japanese snipers killed Lennard while he huddled under the wing of his plane.

In 1948 his remains were recovered by Australian authorities from a grave on Halmahera Island. On March 10, he was laid to rest at the Galela War Cemetery on Ambon Island with full military honors.

So, the *Sea Horse* story, the gallant thoroughbred and the men who brought it alive, is complete. On occasion, I bring out the tattered photo album and drift back to the 1940s to hang with the P-399 crew during the best years of their lives.

—George D. Jepson

Acknowledgments

No book gets written without assistance from unsung individuals. We were lucky to have the support from our families and friends from the outset. Along the way, there were others whose contributions were critical to *Crash Boat* appearing in print.

Near my desk is a scale model of the *Sea Horse* crafted by Al Ross II, master modeler and the author of several books, including the two-volume history *Allied Coastal Forces of World War II* written with John Lambert. The model is a material reminder of the P-399 and its crew. Al read early and late drafts of the manuscript and offered helpful suggestions on content, as well as encouraged us to document the role of air-sea rescue vessels during the war. Al's connection to small combatants dates back to his father Albert P. Ross's service aboard PT 34 in Motor Torpedo Boat Squadron Three in the Philippines.

Many thanks to Tom McCarthy, award-winning ghost writer and editor, for his confidence in *Crash Boat* after reading an early draft and seeing it through the acquisition process at Lyons Press. Huzzahs for Rick Rinehart, executive editor at Lyons Press, for shepherding the manuscript through the production process in the Rowman & Littlefield Publishing Group. And, of course, I am eternally grateful to my wife, Amy, for her support from the beginning, including reading and commenting on virtually every word.

I am indebted to Karen Wales, my editor at *WoodenBoat* magazine, for suggesting that I write an article about the *Sea Horse* for the publication, which appeared in the May/June issue in 2008. Portions of this piece appear in *Crash Boat.*

Two individuals were especially invaluable to Skipper's early work on his memoirs. Jarrell B. Blair, Director of the Augusta Air Museum in Augusta, Kansas, was extremely helpful in gathering information about the War Bond drive, which funded the building of the P-399, and the christening of the vessel. He is the force behind a display at the museum honoring the wartime citizens of Augusta, the *Sea Horse*, and the crew. Thanks is also owed to Donald Rice, Director of Veterans Affairs for Dutchess County, New York, for his kind assistance.

Lastly, I will always remember Skipper's friendship and willingness to take me under his wing during a sensitive period in my life. Every time I hear Duke Ellington's recording of "Take the A Train," a particular favorite aboard the *Sea Horse*, I think of the man whose friendship spanned two generations in our family.

—George D. Jepson

Bibliography

Army Air Force. *Handbook of Instructions for 63-Foot AAF Rescue Boats.* St. Louis: Ross-Gould Company, 1945.

Hess, William. *Pacific Sweep.* New York: Kensington Publishing Company, 1974.

Jepson, George D. "P-399: Sea Horse—A Thoroughbred Goes to War." *WoodenBoat* 202, May/June 2008.

Keegan, John, ed. *The Times Atlas of the Second World War.* London: Times Books Limited, 1989.

Morison, Admiral Samuel Eliot, USNR. *The Liberation of the Philippines.* Boston: Little Brown & Company, 1959.

Ransom, Frank E. *US Air Force Historical Study No. 95: Air-Sea Rescue 1941-1952.* Maxwell AFB: USAF Historical Division Research Studies Institute, 1954.

Rappleyea, George W. *Navigation Wrinkles for Combat Motor Boats.* New Orleans: Higgins Industries, 1945.

Symonds, Craig L. *The Naval Institute Historical Atlas of the US Navy.* Annapolis: The United States Naval Institute Press: 1995.

U.S. Crash Boats: https://uscrashboats.org.

Appendix A

Dair N. Long and the Homegrown War Effort

In 1940, when Dair N. Long and his team at Miami Shipbuilding designed the prototype for the *Sea Horse* and other crash boats, he worked to specifications presented by the British Royal Air Force. The initial orders came in early 1941, and by 1943 more than four hundred boats had been ordered, although fewer were shipped. Several went to South Africa and Russia, the latter for use as small subchasers.

At the time, armed conflict in the Pacific was far off, even as war clouds continued to grow in Europe following Germany's assault on Poland in 1939. But the Japanese attack on Pearl Harbor ignited a response in America down to the country's grassroots. Industry cranked into high gear to produce ships, aircraft, clothing, food, and war matériel (weapons and munitions) at previously unheard of rates to support US and Allied forces around the world.

Small boatyards such as Fellows & Stewart, in Wilmington, California, leaped into the fray and began constructing wooden vessels. Private yards from Maine to California and from Michigan to Florida that specialized in yachts and fishing vessels before the war converted to accommodate construction of the AVR 63s. By war's end in 1945, these yards, with their skilled shipwrights, had launched seventy-nine AVR 63s for the USAAF.

The boat's hull, built upright, was double-planked in cedar inside and mahogany outside, with eight-ounce cotton duck saturated with marine glue between layers. The cedar inner planking ran diagonally at approximately a forty-five-degree angle, while the mahogany outer planking ran longitudinally.

This construction is contrary to the myth that the rescue boats, and the larger PT boats they resembled, were nothing more than plywood speedboats. Underneath the wartime flat gray hulls of both types were the materials and workmanship that rivaled fine sea-going yachts.

In early 1943, while the keel was being laid for the *Sea Horse*, people rallied from all parts of the country to contribute to the war effort. Far from the sea, in the small town of Augusta, Kansas, citizens conducted a War Bond drive to finance the construction of rescue boat P-399 (one of forty-one hulls built by Fellows & Stewart), ultimately collecting seventy-five thousand dollars, including pennies gathered by school children who wanted to contribute.

On July 6, 1943, Miss Ellen Malcom swung a bottle of champagne across the bow of the P-399, officially christening the boat at the Fellows & Stewart yard. Malcom, an employee of Douglas Aircraft in nearby Long Beach, and originally from Augusta, represented the Kansas community. In an open letter to the citizens of Augusta after the ceremony, she wrote: "To good American people like those who bought War Bonds and Stamps to make this ship possible, I send my appreciation and may God Bless America."

This article originally appeared in WoodenBoat *magazine 202 in May/June 2008.*

—George D. Jepson

Dair N. Long's Storied Career

Early in his career, naval architect Dair N. Long caught the eye of Navy brass. In 1938, while a student at the University of Michigan in Ann Arbor, he entered a US Navy–sponsored contest to design a fifty-four-foot and a seventy-foot MTB for experimental purposes. Long did not win the contest, but his entry impressed the Navy.

The winner of the fifty-four-foot MTB design was George F. Crouch, a well-known designer of powerboats. Sparkman & Stephens, the naval architecture and yacht brokerage firm, won the seventy-foot class.

In mid-1939, Miami Shipbuilding Company was awarded the contract for two experimental patrol-torpedo boats (PT 1 and 2) based on Crouch's design, with some modifications by the Bureau of Ships. Miami Shipbuilding hired Long to oversee the application of the design. With the advent of World War II, Long remained at the company and did not return to his studies at Michigan.

The crash boats that served the AAF were procured during World War II under Navy contracts using AAF funds. In addition to designing the sixty-three-foot crash boat, Dair Long also designed an eighty-five-foot air-sea rescue boat that saw action in the Pacific late in the war. This design was built by many of the civilian boatyards that turned out the AVR 63s. Long and Miami Shipbuilding were also involved with designing and building several military craft used by the Office of Strategic Services (OSS) for classified operations during the war.

Long's early exposure to torpedo boats and his work with crash boats prepared him for some interesting peacetime work. In 1947 the Western Boat Building Company of Tacoma, Washington, commissioned Long to design the Fairliner Torpedo powerboat. His design was along the same radical lines as the Hacker and Dee Wite torpedoes of the period.

The Fairliner Torpedo qualified for Class D inboard racing under the American Power Boat Association rules and was his only entry into the small runabout market. In 1947 one of Long's other designs, a Fairliner twenty-six-foot cruiser, served as camera boat to record the lift-off speed and angle of Howard Hughes's HK-1 flying boat (known as the *Spruce Goose*) in Long Beach Harbor.

By the 1950s Dair N. Long Associates, Naval Architects & Marine Engineers, was based in Pasadena, California, and had developed designs for Steelcraft Boats, Inc. motor yachts. During this period Long also designed sailboats and commercial craft and did crash boat and subchaser conversions for private boat owners, including movie star John Wayne.

Long was a member of the Society of Naval Architects and Marine Engineers. He died in the early 1970s.

This article originally appeared in WoodenBoat *magazine 202 in May/ June 2008.*

—George D. Jepson

63-Foot AAF Rescue Boat

(Handbook of Instructions for 63-Foot AAF Rescue Boats)

GENERAL DESCRIPTION (SEE FIGURE 1)

The 63-foot AAF Rescue Boat was a twin screw "V" bottom stepless hydroplane intended for offshore, long-range operations. It could be driven at high speeds under severe weather conditions without excessive pounding and yet remain dry. The construction was of ample strength to withstand the severe operation anticipated. It was powered by two 12-cylinder Hall-Scott "Defender" marine engines, rated at 630 bhp at 2100 rpm. A model 2268 engine was installed to starboard, turning a right-hand wheel, and a model 2269 to port, turning a left-hand wheel, which is the engines rotated in opposite directions, with the propellers turning outboard. These engines had a 24-volt starting, ignition, and generating system. Both engines were fully radio-shielded.

ARRANGEMENT BELOW DECKS (SEE FIGURE 2)

Forepeak—The space forward of the collision bulkhead at frame 4 provided a forepeak to be used for an anchor and chain locker. There was a watertight manhole flush with the deck for access to his compartment.

Crew's quarters—Immediately aft of the forepeak was a crew's quarters in which there were two transom berths and two pipe berths. Hanging lockers were provided in the washroom at the forward end of the crew's quarters.

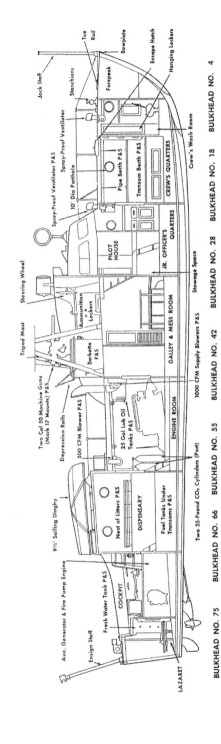

BULKHEAD NO. 75   BULKHEAD NO. 66   BULKHEAD NO. 55   BULKHEAD NO. 42   BULKHEAD NO. 28   BULKHEAD NO. 18   BULKHEAD NO. 4

FIGURE 1 63-foot AAF Rescue Boat
Below Decks Layout AUTHORS' COLLECTION

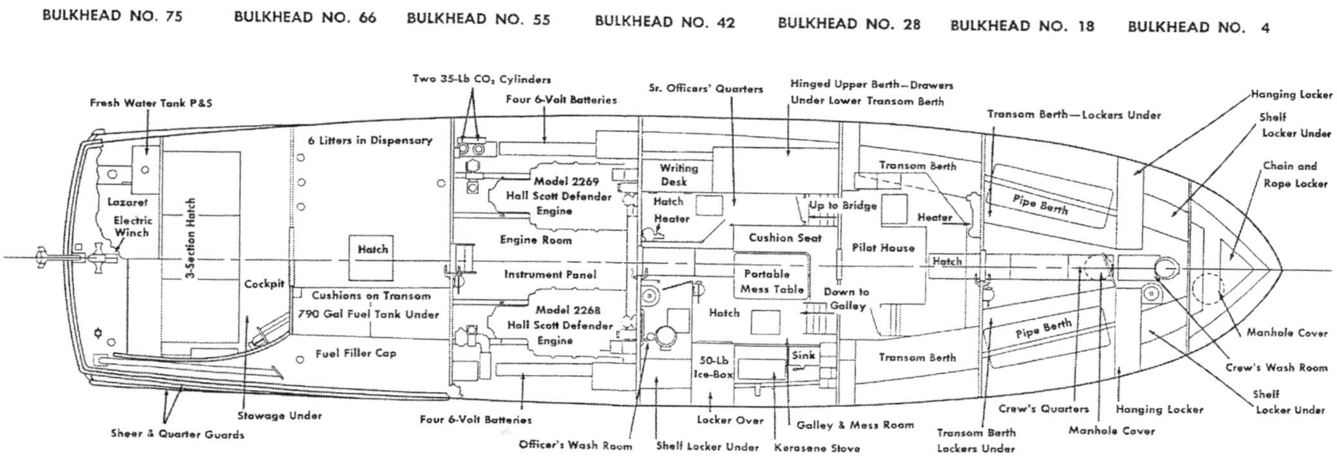

FIGURE 2 63-Foot AAF Rescue Boat
Below Decks Layout AUTHORS' COLLECTION

Jr. Officer's Quarters—Between watertight bulkheads at frames 18 and 28, there were two transom berths with lockers under. Companionways—both port and starboard—led to the pilothouse from these quarters. A passage to starboard led aft from the pilothouse down to the galley, radio room, and officers' quarters. A companionway to port led to the flying bridge and deck. The bulkhead at frame 28 formed the after end of the pilothouse and forward end of the flying bridge.

Galley—The galley, on the starboard side abaft bulkhead 28, was fitted with a 50-pound icebox, three-burner kerosene stove, sink, freshwater pump, disk racks, lockers, and a suction blower for elimination of cooking fumes.

Sr. Officer's quarters—On the port side abaft bulkhead at frame 28, was an officer's stateroom fitted with a transom berth and folding Pullman upper berth, as well as a writing desk, chair, and clothes locker. The officers were provided with a washroom abaft the galley.

Engine room—The engine room was located between the watertight bulkheads at frames 42 and 55.

Dispensary and fuel tank compartment—Beneath the transom berths in the dispensary were two bullet-sealing integral fuel cells. The construction was such that the tanks could be removed and replaced in case they were damaged. The bulkheads at frame 66 were provided with a wide plywood door to facilitate carrying litter in and out of the dispensary.

Cockpit—Aft of the dispensary was an open cockpit for rescue operations. A hatch was provided in the cockpit deck for access to the storage space below.

Lazaret—The freshwater tanks and tiller arms were located in the lazaret, which was between bulkhead 75 and the transom. A hatch in the cockpit seat was provided for access to this compartment.

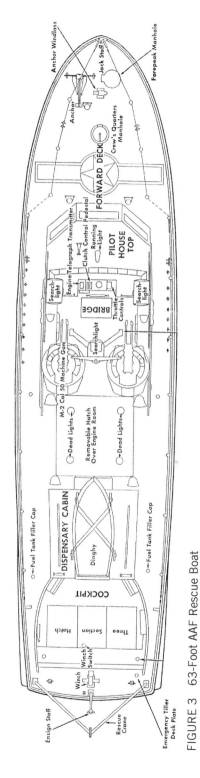

FIGURE 3 63-Foot AAF Rescue Boat
Deck Layout AUTHORS' COLLECTION

Leading Particulars

Dimensions (see Figure 2)
Length, overall...63 ft, 0 in
Length, designed waterline...58 ft, 10 in
Maximum beam (moulded)..15 ft., 0 in
Beam, designed waterline ....13 ft, 10 in
Maximum draft (propeller tips)..3 ft, 10 in
Depth, amidships at centerline to main deck................................8 ft, 9 in
Freeboard forward ....6 ft, 8 in
Freeboard aft to center of deck..4 ft, 7 in

Displacement
Light load displacement (less armament)...............................39,000 lbs
Full load displacement (with armament).................................52,000 lbs

Tank capacities
Fuel gasoline capacity (two tanks) totals........................... 1,580 US gal
Lubricating oil capacity (two tanks) totals............................. 50 US gal
Fresh water capacity (two tanks) totals.........................   150 US gal

Performance
Maximum speed (with full load and complement)..... 33.5 nautical mph
Fuel consumption (full power) .... 110 gal per hr
Fuel consumption (25 knots)... 70 gal per hr

Cruising range
At full speed .... 475 nautical miles
At 25 knots... 530 nautical miles
At 15 knots... 600 nautical miles
Tactical diameter (full speed)... 75 yd
Note: Speeds in excess of 40 nautical mph were attained over measured distances by the P-399 during trials in California and off Guadalcanal.

Index